Rights of the Child

Editor: Danielle Lobban

Volume 412

independence
educational publishers

First published by Independence Educational Publishers

The Studio, High Green

Great Shelford

Cambridge CB22 5EG

England

© Independence 2022

Copyright

Photocopy licence

ISBN-13: 978 1 86168 871 2

Printed in Great Britain

Zenith Print Group

Contents

Introduction

Rights of the Child is Volume 412 in the **issues** series. The aim of the series is to offer current, diverse information about important issues in our world, from a UK perspective.

ABOUT RIGHTS OF THE CHILD

It is a sad fact that children around the world are often at high risk of exploitation and abuse. This book explores why children's rights matter and what those rights are. It also looks at the ways in which the rights of children are violated, focussing on child labour, child marriage, digital privacy and access to education.

OUR SOURCES

Titles in the **issues** series are designed to function as educational resource books, providing a balanced overview of a specific subject.

The information in our books is comprised of facts, articles and opinions from many different sources, including:

♦ Newspaper reports and opinion pieces

♦ Website factsheets

♦ Magazine and journal articles

♦ Statistics and surveys

♦ Government reports

♦ Literature from special interest groups.

A NOTE ON CRITICAL EVALUATION

Because the information reprinted here is from a number of different sources, readers should bear in mind the origin of the text and whether the source is likely to have a particular bias when presenting information (or when conducting their research). It is hoped that, as you read about the many aspects of the issues explored in this book, you will critically evaluate the information presented.

It is important that you decide whether you are being presented with facts or opinions. Does the writer give a biased or unbiased report? If an opinion is being expressed, do you agree with the writer? Is there potential bias to the 'facts' or statistics behind an article?

ASSIGNMENTS

In the back of this book, you will find a selection of assignments designed to help you engage with the articles you have been reading and to explore your own opinions. Some tasks will take longer than others and there is a mixture of design, writing and research-based activities that you can complete alone or in a group.

FURTHER RESEARCH

At the end of each article we have listed its source and a website that you can visit if you would like to conduct your own research. Please remember to critically evaluate any sources that you consult and consider whether the information you are viewing is accurate and unbiased.

Useful Websites

www.allaboutlaw.co.uk

www.bylinetimes.com

www.dandc.eu

www.firstpost.com

www.humanium.org

www.inews.co.uk

www.kidsrights.org

www.metro.co.uk

www.news.un.org

www.ohchr.org

www.positive.news

www.savethechildren.org.uk

www.telegraph.co.uk

www.theconversation.com

www.unherd.com

www.unicef.org.uk

www.voices.ilo.org

www.voice-online.co.uk

www.walesonline.co.uk

www.worldvision.org.uk

Child rights and why they matter

Every right, for every child.

Children and young people have the same general human rights as adults and also specific rights that recognize their special needs. Children are neither the property of their parents nor are they helpless objects of charity. They are human beings and are the subject of their own rights.

The Convention on the Rights of the Child sets out the rights that must be realized for children to develop to their full potential.

The Convention offers a vision of the child as an individual and as a member of a family and community, with rights and responsibilities appropriate to his or her age and stage of development. By recognizing children's rights in this way, the Convention firmly sets the focus on the whole child.

The Convention recognizes the fundamental human dignity of all children and the urgency of ensuring their well-being and development. It makes clear the idea that a basic quality of life should be the right of all children, rather than a privilege enjoyed by a few.

The importance of children's rights

There are many reasons for singling out children's rights in a separate human rights Convention:

Children are individuals

Children are neither the possessions of parents nor of the state, nor are they mere people-in-the-making; they have equal status as members of the human family.

Children start life as totally dependent beings

Children must rely on adults for the nurture and guidance they need to grow towards independence. Such nurture is ideally found from adults in children's families, but when primary adult caregivers cannot meet children's needs, it is up to the State as the primary duty bearer to find an alternative in the best interests of the child.

The actions, or inactions, of government impact children more strongly than any other group in society

Practically every area of government policy – from education to public health – affects children to some degree. Short-sighted policy making that fails to take children into account has a negative impact on the future of all members of society.

Children's views should be heard and considered in the political process

Children generally do not vote and do not traditionally take part in political processes. Without special attention to the opinions of children – as expressed at home and in schools, in local communities and even in governments – children's views go unheard on the many important issues that affect them now or will affect them in the future.

Many changes in society are having a disproportionate, and often negative, impact on children

Transformation of the family structure, globalization, climate change, digitalization, mass migration, shifting employment patterns and a shrinking social welfare net in many countries all have strong impacts on children. The impact of these changes can be particularly devastating in situations of armed conflict and other emergencies.

The healthy development of children is crucial to the future well-being of any society

Because they are still developing, children are especially vulnerable – more so than adults – to poor living conditions such as poverty, inadequate health care, nutrition, safe water, housing and environmental pollution. The effects of disease, malnutrition and poverty threaten the future of children and therefore the future of the societies in which they live.

The costs to society of failing its children are huge

Social research findings show that children's earliest experiences significantly influence their future development. The course of their development determines their contribution, or cost, to society over the course of their lives.

Know your rights

All children have the same rights.

This is a summary for children of the United Nations Convention on the Rights of the Child.

The rights for children set out here have been agreed by almost every country in the world.

1. You have the rights set out here until you are 18.

2. You have these rights whatever your race or skin colour, whether you are a boy or a girl, whatever language your speak, whatever your religion, political beliefs, nationality or ethnic group, whether you are rich or poor, and whether you are disabled.

3. Whenever adults make decisions or do anything that affects you, they should always think about what is best for you.

4. Your government is responsible for protecting your rights.

5. Your family is responsible for helping you to achieve your rights. Your government should support them to do this.

6. You have the right to live. Your government should make sure you have the chance to survive and develop healthily.

7. You have the right to a name and a nationality, and the right to know and be cared for by your parents.

8. You have the right to an identity – an official record of your name, nationality and family.

9. You have the right to live with your parents, unless that would be bad for you. If your parents are separated, you have the right to have contact with both of them, unless that could be harmful for you.

10. If you live in a different country from your parents, you have the right to move so that you can live together as a family.

11. Your government should take steps to prevent you being taken out of your country illegally.

12. When important decisions are being made that affect you, you have the right to give your opinion and to be taken seriously.

13. You have the right to find out information and to share your ideas through writing, speaking, drawing or any other way, unless it may harm you or anyone else.

14. You have the right to think for yourself, to choose what you believe and to practise your religion, provided this does not stop other people enjoying their rights. Your parents should support and guide you in these matters.

15. You have the right to set up or join a group and to meet together, provided this doesn't stop others enjoying their rights.

16. **You have the right to a private life**, and your character and reputation should not be attacked.

17. **You have the right to get information** that is suitable and beneficial for you from around the world through tv, radio, newspapers, social media and the internet.

18. **Both of your parents are responsible** for bringing you up and should think about what is best for you. Your government should make sure there is support to care for you, particularly if both your parents are working.

19. **You have the right to be protected from violence**, abuse or neglect by your parents or anyone else who cares for you.

20. **If your parents are not able to look after you properly**, your government should arrange for you to be cared for by someone else who will respect your culture, religion and language.

21. **If you are adopted, your needs should be the priority**, whether you are adopted in your country or taken to another country.

22. **If you had to leave your country because you were not safe**, in your new country you have the right to be protected. You should have the same rights as other all children in your new country.

23. **If you have a mental or physical disability**, you should get the education, care and support you need to lead a full and independent life to the best of your ability, and to participate in your community.

24. **You have the right to healthcare** when you are sick and to healthy food, clean water, a clean environment and information to help you stay healthy. Rich countries should help poorer countries do this.

25. **If you are being looked after away from your home**, your situation should be regularly reviewed to make sure you are getting good treatment and care.

26. **You have the right to help from the government** if your family is poor or in need.

27. **You should have the conditions you need** for your physical, mental, spiritual, moral and social development. If your family is unable to provide these conditions, the government should help – particularly with nutrition, clothing and housing.

28. **You have the right to education.** Primary education should be required for all children and should be available free. Secondary education should be available to all children. Higher education should be available according to capacity. School discipline should respect your dignity and your rights.

29. **Your education should help you develop your personality**, talents, and mental and physical abilities. It should encourage you to develop respect in your own culture, for other cultures and for the environment. It should help prepare you to live in and contribute to a free society.

30. **You have the right to enjoy your culture**, to practise your religion and to speak your language, whether or not these are shared by the majority of people in your country.

31. **You have the right to rest, play and take part** in cultural and artistic activities.

32. **You should not have to do work that is dangerous**, that is harmful to your health or development, that interferes with your education, or where people take advantage of you.

33. **Your government should take steps to protect you** from taking, producing or distributing dangerous drugs.

34. **You have the right to be protected from sexual abuse** and exploitation, including prostitution and being used in pornography.

35. **Your government should act to make sure you are not kidnapped**, sold or taken to another country to be exploited.

36. **You should be protected from any other activities** that may harm your wellbeing and development.

37. **If you commit a crime and are given a prison sentence**, you have the right to keep in touch with your family. You should not be treated cruelly or put in a prison with adults. The death penalty and life imprisonment are not allowed for children.

38. **If you are under 15, you should not have to join the army** or fight in a war. Children living in war zones should be given special protection.

39. **If you have been abused**, cruelly treated or affected by war, you should be given special care to help you recover.

40. **If you are accused of breaking the law**, you should be treated fairly and in a way that respects your dignity. Your age should be taken into account. Prison sentences should only be given where children have committed the most serious crimes.

41. **These rights are a minimum.** If the laws in your country give you stronger rights than those outlined here, then those laws should be followed.

This is our summary for children of the United Nations Convention on the Rights of the Child.
The full version of the Convention is here:
https://www.unicef.org.uk/wp-content/uploads/2010/05/UNCRC_united_nations_convention_on_the_rights_of_the_child.pdf

KidsRights Index: 'Devastating impact of global pandemic on children worldwide'

KidsRights Foundation has published its annual KidsRights Index and revealed that the negative impacts of the global pandemic on children across the world is far worse than first feared.

This is a summary for children of the United Nations Convention on the Rights of the Child.

The KidsRights Index is the first and only global ranking of 182 countries worldwide that annually measures how children's rights are respected, and to what extent countries are committed to improving the rights of children. This is the ninth consecutive edition of the Index, and to reflect on an exceptional year, a special note is published alongside to assess the true impact of the Coronavirus on the children of the world.

The KidsRights Foundation founder and Chairman is Marc Dullaert, former Chairman of the European Network of Ombudsmen for Children. Marc said: 'With the ongoing global pandemic, we had to address the devastating impacts and outcomes of COVID-19, and it has unfortunately exceeded our predictions at the outset last year.

'Apart from patients of the Coronavirus, children have been hardest hit, not directly by the virus itself, but fundamentally failed through the deferred actions of governments around the world, despite the signals, which will lead to serious, long-term repercussions for the health of future generations'.

'The full extent of this impact is yet to manifest itself, we are not there yet, and governments will need measures and policies long into the future to deal with this post-COVID-19 crisis.'

The special Index note highlights four key impacts of the pandemic in relation to children: violence against children; non COVID-19 vaccinations for children; education and the related issue of school meals; and mental health and wellbeing.

Marc Dullaert said: 'Global governments must focus on mental health and education as much as the economy in their post-COVID-19 crisis policies to safeguard future generations. Educational recovery is the key to avoiding generational catastrophe.'

Impact on education

It found that: 'schools for more than 168 million children have been closed for almost a full year.' Negative examples include the Netherlands, where the Dutch Government closed schools in December to encourage parents to stay at home. Fewer than half the population in 71 countries have access to the Internet, and this drops below 25% in African and South Asian countries. At least one in three schoolchildren has been unable to access remote learning while their schools were closed. UNESCO has acknowledged that: 'over 100 million additional children will fall below the minimum proficiency level in reading as a result of the health crisis.'

Increase in domestic violence

The report reflects an astonishing increase in domestic violence and abuse during the lockdowns, with children as victims. Evidence from school closures already suggests an increase in early marriage and sexual violence in some countries. The NGO Plan International suggests an additional 13 million child marriages are likely to occur between 2020 and 2030.

Crisis in mental health and wellbeing

An additional 142 million kids fell into material poverty and lack access to social protection, and a report by UNICEF and the International Labour Organization states that every one percentage point rise in poverty leads to at least a 0.7 percentage point increase in child labour.

Losing access to school meals, often the main or most nutritious meal of the day, has serious consequences for children's physical development and mental wellbeing, with 370 million kids missing out in the pandemic. In March 2021, in Latin America and the Caribbean alone, 80 million children were still reported to be without daily school meals. In the UK, the Royal College of Psychiatrists identified in April that while the crisis is affecting people of all ages, it is under 18s who are suffering most with mental health issues. They identified: 'the devastating effect that school closures, disrupted friendships and the uncertainty caused by the pandemic have had on the mental health of our children and young people.' The report also acknowledges Manchester United and England striker Marcus Rashford's

role in maintaining and extending free school meal services for 'disadvantaged' children in the UK.

Positive actions

There were some rare rays of light over the past year. Bangladesh, despite widespread poverty, led an initiative to home school by taking over one of the national TV channels, Bangladesh Television. And both Belgium and Sweden are highlighted as doing their utmost to keep schools open in their countries. Scotland will become the first devolved nation in the world to directly incorporate the UN Convention on the Rights of the Child into domestic law. The Scottish Government adopted several poverty alleviation measures quickly in response to the pandemic, and is also unique in using Child Rights Impact Assessments for all Coronavirus policy interventions that might have a bearing on children.

The KidsRights Foundation consulted with Children's Ombudspersons across Europe and found that European governments showed insufficient priority for children and their rights in their Coronavirus policies and response measures.

Recommendations for action

To help policy makers with meaningful follow-up actions, the UN Committee on the Rights of the Child has produced a framework of child rights-based principles and directions (Annex A).

Governments are morally obliged to adopt a Covid Child Rights Impact Assessment (CRIA) for all their current and future Covid and post-Covid policies, and should prioritise this in order to safeguard the rights of future generations, and to avoid a generational catastrophe.

KidsRights Index Report

The annual KidsRights Index is based on the nearly universally ratified United Nations Convention on the Rights of the Child (CRC), and provides a general overview of country performance on children's rights. It also creates a basis for making concrete evidence-based recommendations on how governments might improve on various aspects of children's rights. The Index domains are: Right to Life; Right to Health; Right to Education; Right to Protection; and Enabling Environment for Child Rights.

Industrialised countries score low on best available budget

The KidsRights Index 2021 shows that countries are not allocating sufficient budget for the realisation of children's rights. None of the countries which received their new concluding observations in 2020 scored highest for the indicator 'best available budget/resources'. It is also noteworthy that, on average, industrialised countries scored lowest on this indicator.

The African continent scores highest on the best interest of the child.

The African continent ranked highest of the continents in Domain 5, Enabling Environment for Child Rights.

Austria and Hungary score low on discrimination

The KidsRights Index 2021 shows high levels of discrimination within countries, despite the advent of Black Lives Matter over the past year. No country achieved the highest possible score for the indicator on non-discrimination, and over 60% of the countries received the lowest.

Big fallers from last year's Index include Austria and Hungary, both scoring badly on discrimination. Hungary falls 97 ranks to 144, with discrimination against Roma children of particular concern. Paraguay jumps 66 places largely as a result of a 45% reduction in maternal mortality rates, while Bahrain and Singapore climb 30 and 20 places respectively through the registration at birth of all children in the country.

UK and Australia score low compared to HDI ranking

Thailand, Latvia and Kazakhstan rate more highly than the likes of China, Hong Kong, the UK, Australia and New Zealand in the priority they show for the needs of their young people. For example, Australia ranks eighth in the Human Development Index (HDI) yet is at 135 in the KidsRights Index; while the UK is 13th on HDI, yet down in 169th place on the KidsRights Index.

In summary, the countries that are doing well overall in achieving economic growth or human development are not necessarily also doing well in their capacity to meet their obligations under the CRC.

In 2021, Iceland continues to top the KidsRights index, with 'expected years of schooling' of 18 years for boys and 20 years for girls, followed by Switzerland and Finland; Sierra leone, Afghanistan and Chad occupy the final three places, with boys in Chad having less than nine years of schooling, and girls six.

State of Palestine included for first time

The State of Palestine is included in this year's KidsRights Index for the first time. The country's overall position is 104, with a relatively high ranking of 11 in the Domain of Health, where Palestine has done well on various accounts: 99% of the children are immunized and 'only' 1.4% of children remain underweight. But the Committee also noted the persistent discrimination against children from Bedouin communities and against girls.

KidsRights is an international non-governmental organization that promotes the wellbeing of very vulnerable children across the world and advocates the realisation of their rights. The KidsRights Index is produced in cooperation with Erasmus University Rotterdam, Erasmus School of Economics, and the International Institute of Social Studies. It sits alongside the Foundation's prestigious and acknowledged International Children's Peace Prize, endorsed by the Nobel Peace Laureates, whose recipients have included Malala Yousafzai.

3 June 2021

KidsRights Index Overall Ranking 2021

In 2021, Iceland continues to top the KidsRights index.

Table 1. Top ten of the KidsRights Index 2021

Rank KRI 2021	Countries/182	Score KRI 2021
1	Iceland	0.966
2	Switzerland	0.937
3	Finland	0.934
4	Sweden	0.915
5	Netherlands	0.909[1]
6	Germany	0.909
7	Slovenia	0.899
8	France	0.892
9	Denmark	0.891
10	Thailand	0.889

[1]Differences in ranking within a cluster, despite having the same score, is because the ranking is based on the complete score received up to 15 decimal points. However, for the purpose of representation, the scores are only shown up to a rounded figure of 3 decimal points.

Table 2. Bottom eleven of the KidsRights Index 2021

Rank KRI 2021	Countries/182	Score KRI 2021
182	Chad	0.146
181	Afghanistan	0.198
180	Sierra Leone	0.218
179	Democratic Republic of the Congo	0.273
178	Papua New Guinea	0.275
177	Equatorial Guinea	0.281
176	Central African Republic	0.290
175	Guinea	0.312
174	El Salvador	0.331
173	Guinea-Bissau	0.355
172	Nigeria	0.356

The complete rankings and rankings per domain are available at www.kidsrightsindex.org

www.kidsrights.org

Source: KidsRights

Children march for their rights in Scotland

Scottish ministers have promised to enshrine children's rights into law – kids marched to Holyrood to remind them of their pledge.

By Gavin Haines

Scottish ministers have promised to enshrine children's rights into law – kids marched to Holyrood to remind them of their pledge

On a chilly November morning, children from across Scotland travelled to Edinburgh to take over the Scottish Parliament and talk to ministers – or as 11-year-old Rory put it: 'We just kind of snatched MSPs and said "listen to us!".'

The friendly takeover was timed to mark the 30th anniversary of the United Nations Convention on the Rights of the Child (UNCRC), which acknowledges that every child has the right to life, the right to their own identity, and the right to express opinions and have them heard.

The UNCRC remains the most widely ratified human rights treaty, but millions of children are still waiting for its promises to be fulfilled, including many in Scotland. First Minister Nicola Sturgeon has pledged to enshrine the UNCRC in law by 2021, which would make Scotland a world leader in children's rights.

Among those marching to Holyrood were members of the Children's Parliament, a charity that gives children from all backgrounds the opportunity to share their experiences of growing up in Scotland to influence positive change in their homes, schools and communities.

'The majority of the children we work with in our programmes, projects and consultations are referred by teachers, social workers or youth workers,' said Cathy McCulloch, co-director of the Children's Parliament. 'It's wonderful to see the penny drop when children realise they are valued and respected.'

Members of the Children's Parliament are encouraged to examine various social issues through the lens of storytelling and play, and to present their findings to the relevant decision makers.

'We just snatched MSPs and said "listen to us!".'

'We had a project in Edinburgh where children worked with the council to embed children's rights into local services, looking at what kind of Edinburgh would enable children to grow up happy, healthy and safe,' said Katie Reid, children's voices project worker.

Haris, 11, was one of the children who took part in the project, which highlighted poverty, smoking near schools and 'shouty teachers' as obstacles to children's rights. 'Poverty is a big thing that can stop you going to school and doing the best thing you can do,' he said, adding that he'd like to see smoking bans enforced near schools. 'Outside our school there are quite a few smokers.'

Asked what it would mean to have the UNCRC adopted into Scots law, 10-year-old Folake, who is also a member of the Children's Parliament, said simply: 'We are going to have a happier life.'

18 February 2020

Children's right to privacy in the digital age must be improved

A new report presented to the Human Rights Council says that maximising children's privacy in the digital age means acting in their best interests, actively seeking children's views and treating those views seriously.

Today's children are the first generation to be born into a digital age, while their parents are the first to rear 'digital children,' according to a new report.

How this affects their privacy, as well as their development, is examined by the Special Rapporteur on the right to privacy, Joseph Cannataci, in the final report of his six-year mandate.

The two-themed report, also looking at the issue of artificial intelligence and privacy, was presented to the 47th Session of the Human Rights Council.

'Threats to children's privacy, both in the digital space and out of it, are increasing at alarming rates,' says Cannataci. 'Parents have a role to play in protecting their children's right to privacy, but it is not only up to them: States must safeguard children's rights by establishing appropriate practices and laws, and also ensuring information is available to children themselves on exercising their rights.'

The report details that children's use of social media doubles between the ages of nine and 12, with some 40 percent of them having multiple social media profiles. On average, a teenager's online contacts double during secondary school.

More and more, according to the report, a child's digital identity commences before birth with in-utero images shared by parents and families across the web, many of which are embedded with personal information.

Some 80 per cent of children living in developed Western countries have a digital footprint before they are two years old, largely due to the actions of their family members.

COVID-19 increasing children's online presence

The report notes that the COVID-19 pandemic has even further expanded children's presence on social media, with, for example, daily active accounts for Facebook's Messenger Kids growing by 350 per cent from March to September 2020.

School closures, affecting around 90 percent of the global student population, led to an enormous shift to online learning. Downloads of education applications increased 90 percent compared to the weekly average in late 2019.

'This amplified existing power imbalances between education technology companies and children, and between governments and children and parents, with several governments waiving existing child data privacy laws,' noted Cannataci.

Children more vulnerable in the online space

Of great concern, according to the report, is the digitalisation and storage of children's learning data including thinking characteristics, learning trajectory, engagement score, response times, pages read and videos viewed.

An expanding online world for children provides benefits, but also risks such as online sexual abuse and collection of their personal information, particularly for the online advertising market. It means marketers can target younger children, who are not able to differentiate between advertising and content or between fiction and reality.

These risks, says Cannataci, 'can limit their potential self-development in childhood, adolescence and possibly adulthood. At its worst, they can severely harm their mental and emotional health and physical well-being.'

A human rights approach is required

Countering such abuse requires strategies based on human rights, says Cannataci. The digital space can have many benefits to children's development particularly for exploring creativity and self-expression. At the same time, he says that children must be able to enjoy their rights to unhindered development of personality without being impaired by commercial practices.

The expert highlights childrens' right to education on healthy sexual relationships, consent, and safe practices which can help children protect and advance their privacy, autonomy, and facilitate wellbeing, particularly for LGBTQI youth.

Cannataci urges governments, companies, communities, individuals and parents to recognise children as individuals and therefore the bearers of rights and freedoms. In order to maximise the positive aspects of the digital sphere, while at the same time addressing abuse, says Cannataci, human rights approaches must be used. It is also important to actively involve children in conversations about these approaches, as well as families, communities, governments, civil society and the private sector.

The report also promotes greater attention to privacy engineering in technologies, and wider 'digital literacy education' to enable children and their families to navigate technologies in thoughtful, rights respecting and safe ways.

However, concludes Cannataci, 'technical solutions and digital literacy alone are insufficient without rigorous and sustained action by States to address structural inequities and ensure children's privacy, data protection and safety.'

15 July 2021

Digital emancipation: What are the rights of children of the Instagram age?

Babies born today will, most likely, make their Instagram debuts from being just a few hours old. But what happens when they realise a traceable archive of their childhood exists on their parents' social media?

By Elizabeth Hurst

The first generation of children to have their earliest moments plastered over Facebook have grown up. With this, there have been a few isolated instances of children objecting to what their parents have posted about them –so much so that they have taken the matter to court.

In a landmark case from 2016, a woman in Austria sued her parents in order to force them to remove childhood pictures of her from Facebook. The unnamed 18-year-old stated that the pictures were embarrassing and a violation of her privacy, telling Austria's Heute newspaper: 'They knew no shame and no limits... they didn't care if I was sitting on the toilet or lying naked in the cot, every moment was photographed and made public.'

On the other side of the debate, her father told her that as he had taken the photographs, he had the right to do with them as he pleased. More than 500 pictures of the woman were shared on Facebook to around 700 friends, leading to her suing her parents for infringing on her right to privacy.

The 2016 Austrian court case is an extreme example of the wider movement of people, especially young people, not trusting social media. A study found that 34% of Generation Z (defined as those born from the mid-1990s to early 2000s) say they're permanently quitting social media, and 64% are taking a break from it.

The research also discovered that 41% of young people are made to feel anxious, sad or depressed by social media

platforms like Facebook, Instagram and Snapchat. These 'social natives' have never known anything but the world of social media, and thus their childhoods have been greatly impacted by it, often without their expressed permission.

Parents make many decisions for their kids that undoubtedly have effects on them later in life. After all, a baby can't tell you whether it prefers breast milk over formula, what name it likes... or opt in to being featured on your Instagram. But in the case of choosing whether to put images of your children on social media, the long term consequences are yet to be discovered.

The rise of smartphones and social media have undoubtedly changed almost every element of modern life, including how families interact with each other. In the UK, a recent survey undertaken in conjunction with Parent Zone found that by the time a child turns five, the average parent will have posted 1,498 pictures of them on social media. The survey also found that 85% of parents had not reviewed their Facebook privacy settings in more than a year, and 79% wrongly believed that strangers could not see pictures of their children. More than a third of parents even admit that over 50% of their Facebook friends are only online friends who they would not call a 'true friend', or say hello to if they bumped into them on the street.

Though it may seem innocent for parents to post a few pictures of their offspring, there are many potential issues that can have both short and long-term effects. One is the possible mental health implications of exposing children to social media at an early age. 'It's certainly an issue which I have seen increasingly in my practice over recent years and it is a cause of concern and anxiety for teens,' said Genevieve von Lob, a psychologist and author of *Happy Parent, Happy Child: 10 Steps to Stress-free Family Life*.

'It's understandable that as parents we adore our kids and love to share as much about them as possible,' von Lob said. 'But by sharing endless pictures, you are creating a 'digital tattoo' that could stay with them for the rest of their lives.'

There are many reasons why children might later object to this 'digital footprint'. When they become teenagers, this material may be accessible by their peers, and provide a source for bullying. As they get older, it can cause embarrassment.

Do they really want future friends, partners, university admissions boards, co-workers and potential bosses to be able to look through their online photo albums? Many millenials are now seeing photographs and posts (thanks to apps like Timehop and Facebook's 'On this day' feature) that they shared in their teenage years. They are a mixture of amused and mortified – but whereas the cringe-worthy statuses posted in your youth can be easily deleted, it's a completely different story when the material was posted without your knowledge, and is out of your control.

There are also some darker implications to consider. Though you can make use of social media privacy settings, sharing something online always has the inherent risk that it is accessible to people that you may not want to see it. Though you may proudly post photographs of your toddler potty training, in the bath or happily playing naked on the beach, as Pink did on her Instagram to general outrage,

there is always the chance that people may see and use these images not-so-innocently.

As facial recognition software advances, the ability to create deepfakes is becoming easier and social credit systems have been developed in countries like China, one could argue that the less information about you online, the better. At the very least, it should be up to the person themselves to decide for themselves, instead of having that decision taken away by a parent or guardian.

Currently, France leads the way in legally preventing future harm to children because of their parents' online choices. Under French privacy law, anyone who publishes and distributes images of someone else without their explicit consent – including parents posting pictures of their own children – can face up to one year in prison or a fine of up to €45,000 (£38,000).

The law rests on the principle that the images you post of a non-consenting child will endure in the future, and thus may distress or shame the child in the years to come. This law was promoted in 2016 by a viral online campaign [that] urged parents to cut back on posting images of their children, as the French police suggested that they could attract sexual predators, and one legal expert even warned that parents may face future lawsuits from their kids for violating their privacy.

There is currently nothing explicit within UK law that prevents parents from posting images of their children online. In theory, Article 8 of the Human Rights Act 1998 could be applied in this situation. It describes the right to private and family life, namely the right that protects your dignity and autonomy (your right to be independent and make your own decisions about your life), including the respect for your private and confidential information, the

storing and sharing of data about you, and the right to control the spreading of information about your private life, including photographs taken covertly.

Assuming that photographs taken of you as a child depict your private life, it follows that this could infringe your right to privacy and the ability to make your own decision on this matter at an age when you are able to understand it.

The United Nations warned in June 2018 that parents who share pictures of their children on social media are putting their human rights at risk. Joseph Cannataci, the UN's special rapporteur, said that 'strong guidelines' were needed to preserve the rights of children whose parents choose to click upload.

He said, 'We've already seen the very first cases of kids suing their parents because of the stuff they have posted on Facebook about them... how do you deal with parents who insist on taking a video of their kids every single day and posting it on Youtube every single day?'

The rise of 'Mummy' influencers and family vloggers provides a case study into just how far this can go. Families can amass millions of followers and earn money just by putting photos and videos of their lives – and their children's lives – online. They can become celebrities in their own right, before their children even understand what a celebrity is.

Though this can be transformative for the children through the wealth and opportunities it can generate, it is not without its potential drawbacks. Parents face scrutiny for their private actions and decisions, as found by popular UK family vloggers The Saccone-Jolys who faced backlash from some of their 1.9 million YouTube subscribers. They were accused of child abuse after disciplining their two-year-old with a cold shower.

How can a child understand the distinction between what moments are for an audience of millions, and what remains private? In some cases, the lines have been blurred. One particular case is that of the YouTube account FamilyOFive in which two parents used their children to make viral prank videos for their 750,000 subscribers. The parents were charged with child neglect, sentenced to five years probation and lost custody of two of their five children. Though the parents claimed that the children were 'acting' in the pranks, the evidence of emotional and physical harm was broadcast for all to see.

Parenting coach Ray FitzGerald who runs the site 'Raise a Legend' and doesn't post his daughter's name or age online tells his audience to follow the 'three P rules of posting'. These include privacy ('Make sure your privacy settings aren't public. Treat your child's private images like your Social Security number and don't hand it out like digital candy'); perception ('If you wouldn't want a similar picture of yourself shared, then you likely shouldn't share one of your child'); and permission (a rule he admits mostly applies to older kids). While these alliterative rules are easy to remember and make sense, it begs the question –why don't explicit laws exist to protect our children's right to privacy online?

What do mum and dad think?

Ben, dad to Arden (6 months)

I'm a proud parent but I don't post anything –not even words –about my daughter. A combination of (in my opinion) oversharing by other parents and the way privacy and data is handled these days has led me to be more guarded about what I let people into. So I've adopted this stance with how I share my daughter with the world.

I also like her being able to create her own social footprint, and not have people that have never met her – and that includes some estranged friends and family members, not just strangers – feel like they know all about her. We have a couple of private message groups to share cute or landmark moments with close family, but I don't feel comfortable posting this content on Facebook – even if my privacy settings were restricted.

Susannah, mum to Lucas (6)

I don't really use social media as much as I used to but I used to post quite a lot when Lucas was younger. I just make sure I'm private on Instagram and Facebook, and I've narrowed my friends list down to make sure it's just people I know.

As I got older I've realised I'm happy just living my life for myself and not other people whereas in the past – as a younger, less-secure person –I needed likes to feel like I had a good life instead of now just knowing I've got one. It's not that I specifically don't want Lucas on social media any more, it's just I'm happier focusing on spending time with him rather than posting about him. I think a private life is better and safer too as you never know who's looking.

Lucy, mum to Philippa (3) and Jessica (1)

I like sharing the activities I'm doing with the kids or things they have done that have made me smile as I know it brightens my day and others. However, I'm aware that sharing can create problems. I try to only post to people who I'm friends with. On Instagram, my account is private so I can approve who can see my posts. Just to be sure of privacy, I try not to post anything about the kids that would embarrass them. As they are getting older, I'm definitely reducing the amount that I post about them as they start to have their own little identities. I'm also getting a little bit tired of social media, although I do like the memory hops, which of course won't be there for me to look back on if I stop!

One of my frustrations with social media is that people only really share the good stuff and this is especially so for parents and their kids. I try to post some of the reality (although not all) while at the same time being careful of not complaining!

27 May 2020

Why children need to be taught more about their human rights

An article from The Conversation.

THE CONVERSATION

By Carol Robinson, Professor of Children's Rights, Edge Hill University

Many children have an innate sense of equality, fairness and justice and know how these concepts relate to their day-to-day lives. A lot of children also have the confidence to voice their opinions when they feel a lack of justice. But unfortunately, this is not always that case – especially for children whose personal rights are violated and who face mistreatment, often behind closed doors.

A recent report from the Office of the Children's Commissioner estimates that 2.3 million children in England are living with risk because of a vulnerable family background. This includes children in the care system and children known to have experienced personal harm as well as those living in families where there is a high likelihood of harm.

Worryingly, an estimated 829,000 of these children are not known to social services or to children's mental health services so are not receiving any support. Added to this, since the beginning of the COVID-19 pandemic, rates of domestic abuse have increased, meaning even more children may be living in homes where they are at risk of witnessing, or being on the receiving end of, violent behaviour.

Children need to know how to get help when they feel at risk. They also need to understand how rights apply to them and their lives – and while a limited amount of this is done in schools, it currently doesn't go far enough.

Children's rights

Children's rights are a subset of human rights. The United Nations Convention on the Rights of the Child sets out the rights that all children worldwide should have access to and is one of the most widely adopted international treaties of all time.

In England, specific teaching about human rights is included in Relationships Education for primary age pupils and in Relationships and Sex Education for secondary age pupils. Both primary and secondary pupils also learn about human rights in Health Education and in Citizenship education.

As part of these subjects, in primary schools, aspects relating to rights education includes pupils learning to recognise if relationships make them feel unhappy, unsafe or uncomfortable. Pupils also learn how to report any concerns or abuse and where they can get help.

In secondary schools, pupils are taught about issues such as how to recognise when a relationship is unsafe, what constitutes sexual harassment and sexual violence and why these are unacceptable. They are also taught about legal rights and responsibilities regarding equality, online rights, as well as how to report and get advice if needed for themselves or others. Civil liberties enjoyed by the citizens of the UK are also looked at, as are the nature of rules and laws and the justice system.

These subjects include some important teaching about rights, but the focus is on factual information about rights and the help available. What's lacking is teaching children specifically about children's rights and how these rights apply to their own situations. More also needs to be done to empower children with the confidence to voice concerns in cases where their rights are not respected.

Rights Respecting Schools

Unicef UK has developed a Rights Respecting Schools Award. In working towards this award, schools use the Convention on the Rights of the Child to teach pupils about their rights and how these apply in terms of their own lives.

Around 5,000 schools are working through the Unicef award, which equates to about 1.6 million children becoming more aware of their rights. Research shows that children in schools working toward this award develop the confidence to disclose instances where their rights have been disrespected. And this has led to safeguarding issues being identified.

A senior manager in one of the primary schools explained the impact it has made:

We always get some disclosures when we talk about rights at the beginning of the year...the [children] feel empowered to tell someone and that is something that probably wouldn't have happened if it wasn't for this [the award].

But not all children attend schools where the award is on offer. And even when they do, insufficient emphasis is placed on ensuring all pupils are not only made aware of rights and how these apply to them, but have the skills and confidence to act and get help in cases where rights are not respected.

'Know your rights'

Given that under lockdown many children may be spending longer periods of time with adults who may make them feel unsafe and have fewer opportunities to voice these concerns, the need for children's rights education to be incorporated into all levels of schooling is urgent.

The focus needs to be not only on the transmission of knowledge and facts about children's rights but, as asserted by the United Nations World Programme for Human Rights Education, it must also ensure children acquire the skills to apply their rights in a practical way in daily life. And this means teaching children how to take action to defend and promote their rights as and when needed.

3 June 2020

Girls' rights

Girls: Victims of double discrimination.

Written by: Natalia López Translated by: Holly-Anne Whyte Review by: Chihiro Tsukamoto

In many countries, girls are the first victims when children's human rights are violated and they often suffer double discrimination: for their age and for their gender. They are more discriminated against than boys, for being minors and female. Furthermore, this double discrimination can become triple discrimination if one adds other factors, such as being poor or disabled, or belonging to a minority group.

The following facts illustrate the differences between girls and boys:

◆ Girls under five years old are three times more likely to suffer malnutrition than boys under five.

◆ In developing countries, one in three girls do not finish primary education, most often because they spend eight times longer carrying out household tasks. Consequently, there are 96 million illiterate girls aged between 15 and 24, compared to 57 million illiterate boys.

◆ Every day, 25,000 girls are victims of forced marriage. This can mean that they are forced to leave school. Pregnancy is the number one cause of death among 15 to 19-year-old girls.

◆ 50% of sexual assaults in the world involve girls under 16 years old.

Right to life

Girls' right to life is not respected as much as boys'. More boys born have been intentionally carried to full-term and girls die more frequently before the age of five.

There are various factors that contribute to this situation. One is the wish (which is very strong in some countries) to have a son rather than a daughter. This is the case in China where a law limiting parents to having only one child has been introduced. The fact that men are considered more important in the social hierarchy means that many couples choose to terminate a pregnancy if the child would have been a girl.

Likewise, in poorer regions of China and in other countries where it is not possible to find out the sex of the child before it is born, newborn babies are killed when a child of the opposite sex was wanted. This practice is known as infanticide and mainly affects girls (female infanticide).

Both practices have caused a significant imbalance of the sexes in some regions. So much so, that a 2007 report by the UN calculated that there are approximately 100 million less girls than there could have been in the world, 80 million of whom would have come from India and China.

This imbalance has significant long-term consequences. A considerable lack of women in the world could result in a rise in the trafficking of girls and women, or in certain regions, in women being obliged to marry more than one man. It has been calculated that between 2015 and 2030, 25 million men in China will not be able to find a wife.

Right to education

96 million girls are currently illiterate, compared to 57 million boys. This is because in some countries and regions, attending school is not considered a priority for girls. In such places, girls are expected to spend their time on household tasks or helping their mothers care for younger siblings.

Right to health

Few studies on newborns differentiate between boys and girls; however, it seems that girls are born with a slight biological advantage over boys. Nevertheless, in many developing countries this tendency is reversed because girls are more often deprived of medical care, good hygiene, and sufficient nutrition. This means that they are more vulnerable to growth problems and death when they are still very young.

Another serious problem concerning girls' health is child pregnancy. This is a particular problem when pregnancy is the result of a forced marriage and the girl is still too underdeveloped to safely carry a child.

Female genital mutilation is another violation of Children's Rights. Every year, approximately 3 million girls and teenagers suffer this practice, which can lead to irreversible health problems and fatal infections.

Right to protection

Girls all over the world are victims of child marriage, forced pregnancy, trafficking and sexual assaults. In fact, 50% of sexual assaults in the world are committed against girls less than 16 years old.

Furthermore, it is important to highlight that domestic violence, which in many places is considered a private matter, is most often suffered by the girls and women of the family.

Child marriage and pregnancy

Every year, 10 million girls worldwide get married before the age of 18. This fact can have serious repercussions on their futures. It can prevent them from completing their education and can put their health at risk if they become pregnant while they are still very young.

Pregnancy is the number one cause of death among 15 to 19-year-old girls. Both the girls' lives and the lives of their babies are at risk because the girls' bodies are not yet mature enough to safely carry a child and they often do not have access to medical care during the pregnancy, birth or post-natal period. Each year, 70,000 teenagers die in developing countries due to complications related to childbirth or pregnancy.

Girls who are married before the age of 18 have a higher risk, both physical and psychological, of suffering domestic violence at the hands of their husbands or other members of their family. This type of violence is mainly a consequence of the male family members' belief that women and girls are inferior and belong to them.

This type of violence is difficult to quantify and avoid, since it usually occurs behind closed doors. In many places it is considered a private problem and many women would not dare to report it. Not enough is done by governments to detect and punish this type of violence.

Sexual abuse and exploitation

Sexual abuse is a coercive act against a person intended to make them carry out sexual behaviour against their will. Sexual abuse can be physical or psychological, and does not always involve physical contact with the victim, for example, when someone is forced to be in pornographic pictures or videos, or as in the case of forced prostitution.

Sexual abuse is an abuse of power and is one of the most harmful types of violence, both physically and psychologically, because it increases the risk of serious health problems such as sexually transmitted diseases, unwanted pregnancies, and psychological damage leading to depression, suicide, drug and alcohol abuse, etc.

80-90% of the abusers are men, while women act as accomplices. According to the Institut International des Droits de l'Enfant [International Institute for Children's Rights], one in five women and one in five men have been the victims of sexual abuse.

Girls in war

Despite what one might think, there are many girls who join armed groups in times of conflict. In fact, it has been calculated that there are 300,000 child soldiers in the world and that 100,000 of them are girls. Most of them enrol because they want food and protection; however, they are often raped or sexually abused, or suffer other types of violence, even after the conflict has ended.

Reviewed 2021

Family separations in Ukraine highlight the importance of children's rights

An article from The Conversation.

By Christina Clark-Kazak, Associate Professor, Public and International Affairs, L'Université d'Ottawa/University of Ottawa

THE CONVERSATION

Given the conscription of men aged 18 to 60 in Ukraine, the majority of Ukrainians fleeing into neighbouring countries are women and children.

Most adult men and many disabled and older people have been left behind. The resulting family separation poses legal and social challenges that need to be addressed in gender- and age-sensitive ways.

Unaccompanied and separated children require specific protection and care because of their developing capacities to care for themselves and inter-generational power hierarchies. That means that most of the time, adults control resources and decision-making, while children have fewer opportunities to advocate for their own choices, well-being and rights.

As the number of children who flee without their families increases, it's not clear whether there's local capacity to respond effectively and appropriately. Even before the Ukraine war, lone refugee youth who arrived in the United Kingdom without family were living unsupervised in hotels and disappearing at a rate of one per week.

'Best interests principle'

The UN Convention on the Rights of the Child – the most widely ratified human rights treaty in the world – requires that all decisions affecting children are guided by what's known as the best interests principle.

This principle is especially important in cases involving separated children, as well as the evacuation of children in institutional care, such as those in hospitals, prisons or orphanages. In fact, Canada has paused all adoptions from Ukraine in line with international guidelines, law and practice.

These safeguards are put in place so that children are not inadvertently taken away from their families when their identities cannot be verified or when their parents' whereabouts are unknown.

Critiques of the German kindertransport, for example – an effort to rescue children from Nazi-controlled territory in the months prior to the outbreak of the Second World War – show how some Jewish children, although saved from persecution by the Nazis, were also in most cases

Legal challenges

As the violence continues and displacement increases in scope and duration, secondary and tertiary migration is taking place, within Europe and to other regions, including to the United States and Canada.

This causes particular legal and immigration challenges, especially for families helmed by women whose male partners are prohibited from leaving Ukraine.

Canadian immigration officials may require a parent travelling with minor children without their spouse to present a copy of the child's birth certificate, a letter of authorization from the other parent and a photocopy of the non-accompanying parent's passport or national identification card.

Such documentation requirements are in accordance with the 1996 Hague Convention on the Protection of Children, aimed at protecting children against cross-border abduction in cases of

permanently separated from their parents and their Jewish identities.

Given the scale and speed of Ukrainian forced migration, adults making decisions on behalf of separated children and those in care should look to the lessons of the past when focusing on the best interests of children.

For example, the recent announcement of evacuation of children with cancer to Sick Children's Hospital in Toronto includes provisions for family members to accompany them.

Temporary protection

European countries and Canada are offering temporary protection, rather than permanent refugee status.

Under the newly announced Canada-Ukraine Authorization for Emergency Travel, Ukrainians and their immediate family members of any nationality are permitted to stay in Canada as temporary residents for up to three years via a three-year open work permit.

But temporary protection offers fewer formal resettlement and integration structures. Reliance on informal networks can result in exploitation and, in extreme cases, forced prostitution and other forms of human trafficking.

In particular, lack of affordable housing or designated shelters can result in people accepting rooms in private homes without a proper vetting process or ongoing oversight.

Due to this extreme dependency on others' hospitality, the private sphere of domestic spaces and unequal gender and age power relations, displaced children, young people and women may be at higher risk of sexual violence or unwaged domestic work.

custody disputes. However, because people fled quickly from Ukraine and because some men who have been conscripted may have died or moved with military units, these documents may not be easy to obtain.

As a result, women and their children could be 'stuck' in the first country of asylum, even if they have extended family support in other countries.

Mental health impacts

Research shows that long-term family separation has severe impacts for mental health. Children and young people, especially girls and older siblings, in single-parent households often take on additional child care, household and paid labour to support their families.

Older people left behind in Ukraine may feel isolated and abandoned.

Violence and migration have different impacts due to age, family status and gender. Policies and programs to address conflict-induced displacement in Ukraine must explicitly take into account the rights of children, including the best interests of the child. They also need to be attentive to gender and family relationships.

20 March 2022

United Nations acknowledges children's right to clean air after global campaign by young people

Unicef has predicted that air pollution will become the leading cause of child mortality by 2050.

By Will Hazell, Education Correspondent

The UN has announced it is to recognise children's right to clean air following a campaign led by young people around the world.

More than 29,000 children called on the committee of the UN Convention on the Rights of the Child (UNCRC) to acknowledge the right.

Currently, nine out of 10 children around the world are breathing toxins that exceed safe levels which can interfere with critical stages of organ development.

Children are more physiologically vulnerable to air pollution than adults based on their smaller relative size and relative faster breathing rate.

The World Health Organisation estimates that in 2016, 600,000 children died from acute lower respiratory infections caused by polluted air, while Unicef has predicted that air pollution will become the leading cause of child mortality by 2050.

In the UK, the issue has risen to particular prominence after a coroner found in 2020 that air pollution 'made a material contribution' to the death of nine-year-old Ella Adoo-Kissi-Debrah in 2013. It was the first time that air pollution had been formally recognised as a cause of a person's death in this country.

The campaign for the UN to recognise the right was organised by a coalition of groups, including the UK-based charity Global Action Plan, gaining support from 29,674 children from across the globe, including in the UK, US, China and India. It was also backed by organisations including London's Great Ormond Street Hospital.

On Wednesday, the vice-chairman to the committee on the UNCRC, Philip D Jaffé, said the world needed an 'air quality revolution'.

Commenting on the campaign, Professor Jaffé said: 'I will do my part and I will do everything I can with my colleagues to support you in what you are doing.'

Clean air will now be included in a forthcoming 'general comment' from the committee – the process by which the UN outlines what is expected of countries in order to honour the convention.

Sonja Graham, the chief executive of Global Action Plan, said: 'Change is more likely to happen now that we have the support of the committee of the UNCRC so this acknowledgment is a brilliant step in the right direction.

'Through the Freedom to Breathe campaign, the children came to recognise that clean air is an essential necessity for life – just like clean water and healthy food – we are thrilled that the UN is acknowledging this too.'

17 November 2021

Child labour

By Vanessa Cezarita Cordeiro

In the last decade, child labour has decreased by 38%; however, 152 million children are still affected and the COVID-19 pandemic has exacerbated the situation. Child labour reaches many different corners across the world, often occurring in various sectors that can have detrimental educational, health and psychological impacts on children's well-being. There are various drivers of child labour such as poverty, armed conflict, inadequate laws and regulations, social inequality, discrimination and ingrained cultural traditions to name a few.

Defining child labour

The International Labour Organization (ILO) defines child labour as 'work that is mentally, physically, socially or morally dangerous and harmful to children; and/or interferes with their schooling by: depriving them of the opportunity to attend school; obliging them to leave school prematurely; or requiring them to attempt to combine school attendance with excessively long and heavy work' (ILO, n.d).

Not all forms of work undertaken by children are considered to be child labour. This varies from country to country and depends on the child's age, the type of work performed, the number of hours put into work, the conditions they work under and whether it interferes with their schooling. There are activities that children can engage in – such as helping their family in the house, or assisting in a family business to earn an allowance during the school holidays – that can be positive for their development and provide children with skills and experience in order to prepare them for adulthood (ILO).

Defining the 'worst forms of child labour'

Under Article 3 of ILO Convention No. 182, the worst forms of child labour are defined as (ILO, 1999):

♦ all forms of slavery or practices similar to slavery, such as the sale and trafficking of children, debt bondage and serfdom and forced or compulsory labour, including forced or compulsory recruitment of children for use in armed conflict;

♦ the use, procuring or offering of a child for prostitution, for the production of pornography or for pornographic performances;

♦ the use, procuring or offering of a child for illicit activities, in particular for the production and trafficking of drugs as defined in the relevant international treaties;

♦ work which, by its nature or the circumstances in which it is carried out, is likely to harm the health, safety or morals of children.

The worst forms of child labour include (ILO):

♦ Child trafficking

♦ Sexual exploitation (which includes pornography and prostitution)

♦ Drug trafficking

♦ Debt bondage (also referred to as bonded labour)

♦ Slavery

♦ Forced labour

♦ Organized child begging

Defining 'hazardous child labour'

Hazardous child labour is defined under Article 3(d) of ILO Convention No. 182 as 'work which, by its nature or the circumstances in which it is carried out, is likely to harm the health, safety or morals of children' (ILO). Child labour is considered hazardous when a child is working in an unhealthy or dangerous environment where they are at risk of falling ill, psychological and physical injury and in some cases, death (ILO).

Hazardous child labour is the largest category of child labour; it is estimated that approximately 73 million children are working in dangerous environments which include the mining, agriculture, manufacturing and construction sector, including work undertaken in bars, nightclubs, restaurants, markets and domestic services. Hazardous working conditions can cause lifelong illnesses that may not develop until later into adulthood (ILO).

Defining 'forced' child labour

Under international law, 'forced' labour is defined as 'work or service which is exacted from any person under the menace of any penalty for its non-performance and for which the worker does not offer himself voluntarily' (Thevenon & Edmonds, 2019).

This can take two forms: (1) children are forced into labour by their parents/caregivers and their parents are aware of their working conditions; (2) children are forced into labour as a result of trafficking, coercion or deceptive recruitment. In relation to the latter category, these children may have migrated alone or were victims of human trafficking, leaving their parents unaware of their working conditions (Thevenon & Edmonds, 2019).

There are three main categories of forced labour (Thevenon & Edmonds, 2019):

♦ Exploitation – which includes slavery, slavery-like practices, forced domestic labour and bonded labour.

♦ Commercial sexual exploitation

♦ State-imposed forced labour

Global estimates of child labour

The global estimates of child labour as reported by the ILO at the beginning of 2020 were 160 million children – 97 million boys and 63 million girls engaged in child labour. Out of the 160 million children, 79 million children were engaged in hazardous work (ILO, 2020).

According to an ILO report from 2019, approximately 9 in 10 children living in Africa, Asia and the Pacific are involved in child labour. Africa is the highest rank continent, where 1 in 5 children are involved in child labour (Thevenon & Edmonds, 2019).

Globally, child labour progress remains uneven. Across Africa, 72 million children are engaged in child labour and 62 million across Asia and the Pacific. 70% of children engaged in child labour globally work in the agricultural sector, predominantly in livestock herding and subsistence and commercial farming (ILO, 2021).

Drivers of child labour

Despite laws and regulations protecting children from child labour, it still exists. Globally, there are numerous reasons children are pushed into work, with poverty being the greatest driving force. The main causes of child labour include:

1. Poverty and unemployment

Children need to support their families and their survival is dependent on them working. This vulnerability is taken advantage of by criminal gangs or traffickers.

2. Inadequate or weak national educational systems

Inadequate or weak national educational systems play a significant role in child labour. Communities that have inadequate educational facilities, including a lack of teachers and resources, create an unstable environment in which children do not have access [to] education, which in turn pushes them towards child labour. Some families are unable to afford school fees, pushing them towards child labour as

a more lucrative use of children's time. Some cultures place less emphasis on girls going to school and prefer that girls are prepared to carry out household tasks (ILO).

3. Ingrained cultural traditions and attitudes surrounding child labour

Various cultural norms and traditions around the world tacitly encourage child labour by promoting the importance of work to a child's development. For example, certain cultures believe that working is important for character and skill development, regardless of the effects this might have on a child's realization of their human rights. Children are expected to follow in their parents' footsteps and learn a particular trade in order to support their families.

Other traditions encourage children to work to pay off debts borne from social occasions and religious events. These widespread and varied manifestations of bonded labour take advantage of children's vulnerable position within wider societies and cultural expectations. In this way, children are often framed as family supporters, rather than dependents.

4. Violation of existing laws and regulations on child labour

5. Inadequate enforcement of laws and regulations

6. Civil or political unrest or natural disasters

Child labour in different sectors

Child labour is prevalent in various sectors including:

1. Agriculture sector

Traditional societal attitudes towards children's participation in agriculture, lack of agricultural technology, the high costs of adult labour and poverty are some of the main drivers of child labour in the agriculture sector. This sector is one of the most dangerous for children in terms of occupational diseases, non-fatal accidents and work-related fatalities (ILO). Not all child participation in the agricultural activity is considered child labour. Tasks which are low-risk, age-appropriate and do not interfere with a child's time (education or leisure) fail to meet the child labour threshold. These activities must be non-hazardous and can often benefit families and communities by providing children with vital social and technical skills as well as enhancing local food security (ILO).

The sub-sectors that exist within the agriculture industry include (ILO):

♦ Fishing

♦ Livestock production

♦ Farming

♦ Forestry

2. Domestic work also referred to as household work

Domestic work can be defined as instances in which a child under the age of 18 years works within the home of their employer to carry out household chores. Whilst the cultural norm is for girls to work inside the house, boys are more likely to work outside the house (i.e. looking after livestock or gardening). Child domestic workers sometimes live in the home of their employers and may or may not get paid for their work (Thevenon & Edmonds, 2019).

3. Factory work, predominantly in the garment and textile sector

In countries such as Zimbabwe, Indonesia, India, Argentina, Brazil and Malawi, factory child labour is prevalent within the tobacco industries (World Vision). More commonly, child labour in factories often relates to the garment industry and is especially prevalent in Asian countries such as Cambodia and Bangladesh. The rise in fast fashion has pushed companies to find cheaper sources of labour, children. Children work at all stages of the supply-chain production from cotton picking, harvesting, yarn spinning and factory work. This is prevalent in countries such as Egypt, Pakistan, China, Thailand, India, Bangladesh and Uzbekistan (Moulds).

4. Industry and manufacturing (which includes working in mining, quarrying and construction)

Child labour in mines and quarries is prevalent in countries such as Mali, Burkina Faso, Ghana, Niger, Democratic Republic of Congo, Nigeria, Sierra Leone, Liberia, Zambia and Zimbabwe (Child Labour Platform & ILO, 2019).

The sub-sectors that exist within the mining industry include (ILO):

♦ Gold mining

♦ Salt mining

♦ Stone quarrying

♦ Artisanal mining

Effects of child labour

Child labour can have a range of both mental and physical health effects on a child that often continue into adulthood, these vary and include long-term health issues due to abuse, injuries, malnutrition, exhaustion, psychological harm or exposure to chemicals, among others. The mental and physical effects vary depending on the sector that children are working in (Dubay, 2021).

♦ **In agriculture,** children are often exposed to working with hazardous toxic fertilizers and pesticides, as well as heavy and dangerous tools or blades (Dubay, 2021).

♦ **In domestic work,** children face the risk of being abused by their employers, working excessively long hours or being isolated from their friends and family (Dubay, 2021).

♦ **In construction,** children face the risk of injury from working with dangerous and heavy loads and lack adequate personal protective equipment (Dubay, 2021).

♦ **In mining,** children are exposed to working with explosives, poisonous chemicals and face the risk of being placed in dangerous environments such as mines which are regularly the source of collapses that can lead to serious injury or death (Dubay, 2021).

♦ **In manufacturing,** children are exposed to unhealthy toxins, hazardous chemicals and poor health and safety working regulations (Dubay, 2021).

Child labour and gender inequality

The involvement of boys in child labour is much higher than

girls, with approximately 11.2% [of] boys in child labour compared to 7.8% of girls. According to the most recent ILO-UNICEF 2020 report on child labour, it is estimated that there [are] 89.3 million children engaged in child labour between the ages of 5–11 years old, 35.6 million between the ages of 12–14 and 35 million between the ages of 15–17 years (ILO, 2020). This gender gap increases with age as girls are more likely to be involved in unpaid and under-reported domestic child labour. In countries such as Congo, Yemen, Nepal, Peru, Mozambique, Chad and Somalia more girls are involved in child labour than boys (Thevenon & Edmonds, 2019).

It is worth noting that statistics estimating the prevalence of girls and boys in child labour across the globe are subject to a few limitations. Primarily, reliable data sources on child participation in work are limited. Further, the definition upon which these estimates are typically based does not include work within children's homes, despite the fact that girls shoulder a disproportionate burden of household labour in many societies. Recent research by the ILO attempting to include this overlooked portion of child labour purports that involvement in household chores for more than 21 hours a week is considered child labour. Once this fact is taken into account, the global gender gap in child labour prevalence is reduced by almost half (ILO).

Child labour in urban and rural settings

It is more common for child labour to occur in rural areas. According to an ILO study in 2020, 122.7 million rural children were involved in child labour and 37.3 million urban children (ILO, 2020). The most common type of child labour is family-based and this accounts for 72% of all child labour. Family-based child labour is often considered hazardous with 1 in 4 children between the ages of 5-11 years engaged in work that is likely to cause harm to their health (ILO, 2020).

Child labour and education

Poverty, being the main driver of child labour, pushes children into work which forces them to leave school early. Globally, one-third of children engaged in child labour are excluded from school and there is a strong correlation between a child's participation in hazardous work and low school attendance (ILO, 2020).

There are several reasons why child labour affects children's education. For example, the work may be very demanding, they are unable to access education or free schooling, an alternative does not exist or their families push them to work as in certain cultures family perceptions around work and gaining money are more important than education (ILO, 2020).

Globally, as of 2020, the percentage of children between the ages of 5–14 years that do not attend school include: 15.5% in Latin America and the Caribbean, 28.1% in Northern Africa and Western Asia, 28.1% Sub-Saharan Africa, 35.3% in Central and Southern Asia and 37.2% in Eastern and South-Eastern Asia (ILO, 2020).

Child labour and migration

Child migration, often accompanied by family members, can lead to new child labour vulnerabilities. One of the most common drivers of child migration is the availability of seasonal work opportunities in agriculture and brick kilns for parents. Unfortunately, children frequently accompany their parents to support their work and increase the household income as for many migrant working families, this extra output is essential (van de Glind, 2010).

Child labour and COVID-19

In the last two decades, significant improvements have been made in the fight to end child labour. However, the COVID-19 pandemic has threatened to undermine these developments and could potentially reverse many years of progress to eradicate child labour. Prior to the pandemic, the amount of children involved had increased by 8.9 million in just four years. This increase is attributed to rising global poverty levels and is expected to continue into 2022 (ILO, 2020).

Due to an increase in unemployment since the pandemic, families are more inclined to push their children into child labour as a coping mechanism. This is further exacerbated by school closures which leave children vulnerable and at a greater risk of child labour. Non-governmental organisations working within the African region have noted that school closures have pushed children into work as they are expected to help look after their families (ILO, 2020).

Eliminating and preventing child labour

In 2019, the International Labour Organization (ILO) in partnership with Alliance 8.7 launched the International Year for the Elimination of Child Labour for 2021. The aim of 2021 is to urge governments to encourage legislative and practical actions towards the eradication of child labour and to achieve Target 8.7 of the United Nations Sustainable Development Goals (ILO, 2021).

Although global progress has been made towards reducing child labour, the lofty target of eliminating the practice by 2025 remains unmet. The response to this persistent challenge must be unified, intersectional and backed by actionable legislation. In particular, minimum working age requirements and their enforcement are a fundamental component of child labour responses.

Beyond legal and regulatory frameworks, governments and civil society must work to design and implement policies which provide families and children with alternative livelihoods, steering them away from the trappings of child labour. These initiatives must ensure that children are at the heart of all decision-making processes, and that any useful interventions are accessible to the children themselves (Thevenon & Edmonds, 2019).

To upscale the fight against child labour, greater research and public awareness campaigns are required. Governments around the world must acknowledge the scale of this challenge, its evolution and the ways in which families and children are hampered by its presence (Thevenon & Edmonds, 2019). Summarily, governments should work to ensure (Thevenon & Edmonds, 2019):

1. The existence of minimum working age legislation and their enforcement
2. The development of tools and mechanisms to monitor child labour
3. Functional public awareness raising campaigns
4. Support to community-led initiatives
5. Greater protection for vulnerable children and families
6. Affordable, fair, quality and accessible education for all
7. The promotion of positive cultural and societal norms against child labour

Last updated on 31 August 2021

References:
Child Labour Platform & International Labour Organization. (2019, May). 'Child labour in mining and global supply chains.'
Council of Europe. (2013, August 20). 'Child labour in Europe: a persisting challenge.'
GPE Secretariat. (2016, June 12). 'Child labour hinders children's education.'
Human Rights Watch. (2021, May 26). 'COVID-19 pandemic fuelling child labour.'
International Labour Organization, Worst Forms of Child Labour Convention, C182, 17 June 1999.
International Labour Organization. 'Causes '.
International Labour Organization. 'Hazardous child labour'.
International Labour Organization. 'The worst forms of child labour'.
International Labour Organization. 'What is child labour'.
International Labour Organization. (2020, June 10). 'Child labour: Global estimates 2020, trends and the road forward. '
International Labour Organization. (2021, January 15). '2021: International year for the elimination of child labour.'
International Labour Organization. 'Child labour in Africa.' International Labour Organization. 'Child labour in agriculture'.
Moulds, J. 'Child labour in the fashion supply chain.'
Thevenon, O., & Edmonds, E. (2019). 'Child labour: causes, consequences and policies to tackle it. ' Organization for Economic Co-operation and Development.
UNICEF., & ILO. (2020). 'COVID-19 and child labour: A time of crisis, a time to act. '
UNICEF. (2021, June 9). 'Child labour rises to 160 million — first increase in two decades.'
Van de Glind, H. (2010, September). 'Migration and child labour exploring child migrant vulnerabilities and those of children left-behind: working paper.'
World Vision. 'What are the dangers of child labour.'
World Vision. 'Where does child labour happen.'

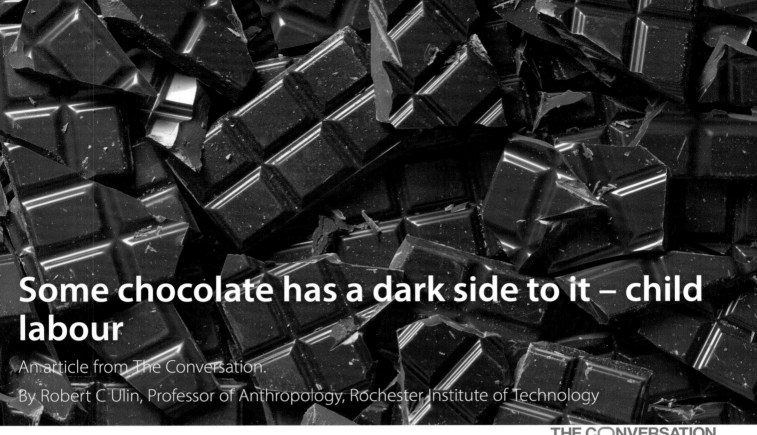

Some chocolate has a dark side to it – child labour

An article from The Conversation.

By Robert C Ulin, Professor of Anthropology, Rochester Institute of Technology

THE CONVERSATION

Chocolate makes for a perfect gift, a comforting snack and even a health food, thanks to its plentiful antioxidants. Rumour has it that it might even work as an aphrodisiac. It is no surprise, then, that the chocolate industry garners billions of dollars each year.

However, there is also a dark side to chocolate.

As a cultural anthropologist who has done years of research on food and drink in Europe and North America, I have come to understand the close relationship between culinary traditions and social inequality.

In a course I teach on the anthropology of food, chocolate is among the numerous food commodities that I cover in the course as an index for understanding social class relations locally and globally, including human trafficking.

Exploitative labour, especially child labour, is among the most troublesome ways in which global chocolate is tied to inequality.

History of chocolate

Chocolate can be traced to the Olmec civilization of Mesoamerica. The Olmec were the first to transform the cacao plant into chocolate, around 1750 B.C. The Olmec used chocolate in religious rituals and as a medicine. It was also used, as anthropologists Sophie D. Coe and Michael D. Coe note, by both the Maya and Aztecs throughout the 15th century.

However, the chocolate used in ritual life was a far cry from the chocolates that we enjoy today. In fact, it was very bitter. Hernan Cortes, the famous Spanish explorer, is said to have brought cacao back to Spain in the early 16th century; there it was mixed with sugar and honey as a drink. It was not until the 17th century that chocolate was consumed throughout Europe, initially among the aristocracy.

The invention of the cocoa press in the 19th century allowed manufacturers to combine sugar with the fatty butter extracted from the beans. The mixture was then poured into moulds and sold, thus ushering in chocolate's popularity among the European masses.

Sugar cane was cultivated by enslaved West Africans in the Caribbean and the Americas as part of the Atlantic trade. Refined sugar cane made its way to England, where it was consumed by the working class as a quick source of energy and a way to satiate hunger.

European goods then made their way to Africa in exchange for slaves, in what anthropologist Sidney Mintz noted in his 1985 book 'Sweetness and Power' as a 'triangle of trade.' It was Caribbean sugar produced by the enslaved West Africans in the 19th century that made chocolate palatable. The connection to slavery does not end here.

Children as cheap slave labour

During the early 19th century, a period marked by colonialism, the British introduced the cacao plants to West Africa, where the growing conditions were ideal. The plants require warmth and humid growing conditions that are common to the tropical forests of the Ivory Coast and Ghana.

The cacao farms are still operating there: mostly small, and with poor owners. Harvesting and processing cacao is labour-intensive and many of these indigent farmers simply do not have the financial means or adequate family labour to make cacao growing viable. And so to economize they turn to children – often as young as 5 but more typically 10 to 12 years in age. The beans are in pods that must be cut open with machetes, making the work quite dangerous, especially for children.

Legal scholar Erika George notes that the vast majority of the children end up on the cacao farms through trafficking. Not all but many of the children come from Mali, especially from very poor rural villages. Reporters have found that many children are approached by traffickers and told that they will earn good wages on the cacao farms. They agree to the work to help their families financially.

As journalist Miki Mistrati shows in the documentary 'The Dark Side of Chocolate,' the traffickers then take the children to the Ivory Coast or Ghana, where they are sold to the farmers. The traffickers themselves are aided by local militia. Children who end up on the farms often work 14- to 16-hour days. They are even expected to carry heavy sacks of beans and beaten if they stumble or collapse.

It is hard to obtain exact figures on the numbers of children who have worked on the cacao farms. The International Labour Organization estimates 1.56 million in the Ivory Coast and Ghana alone

Given the vast financial network involved in the chocolate trade, it is dangerous work for journalists. Mistrati used hidden cameras and passed himself and his companion off as tourists. He mentions a French journalist who disappeared pursuing the story of childhood slavery.

Telling the story

In 2021, six Malian men filed a legal case against Nestle USA and Cargill, claiming that they were trafficked from their villages and forced to labour on cacao farms. The case was brought to the United States Supreme Court with a majority ruling that chocolate companies cannot be sued in the United States for abuse that happened elsewhere, including for child slavery on African farms.

Large chocolate companies may not be participating in the trafficking of children directly, in that they purchase the cacao beans from merchant suppliers. Indeed, eight of the largest chocolate companies signed a protocol in 2001 that condemned child labour and childhood slavery. But it did not commit the industry to put an end to the practice.

Then there are organizations responsible for Fair Trade and the UTZ labels that seek to assure consumers of fair labour practices in the chocolate sector, although this is not an ultimate guarantee that the children have not been exploited in the production process more generally. It should also be noted that the United States Department of Labour has also taken a strong stand against the exploitation of children on cacao farms.

There is a strong argument to be made here against the abuses of labour, especially when it involves children, and to that end we all bear some responsibility as consumers.

16 May 2022

Child servant beaten to death 'for stealing master's fruit'

Police in Pakistan said the 10-year-old boy and his younger brother were tortured for days at their employer's home.

By Ben Farmer

A 10-year-old domestic worker was beaten and tortured to death and his younger brother badly injured after their masters caught them stealing fruit, police said.

Officers said the boys had been tortured for several days at their employers' home in an upmarket neighbourhood of Lahore.

The assaults are the latest to put the spotlight on the exploitation of child labour and young domestic servants in Pakistan.

The issue is feared to have become more severe because of worsening economic conditions, as poverty-stricken families seek to survive by finding jobs for their children.

Police were tipped off by doctors when the boy called Kamran and his six-year-old brother, Rizwan, were brought to hospital with severe injuries.

Kamran was pronounced dead soon afterwards, while Rizwan's condition was critical.

Officers arrested those who had brought the children to hospital, but the owners of the house had fled, the investigating officer told the Telegraph.

The boys were originally from the southern Punjab city of Bahawalpur and had been employed at the home in the Defence Housing Authority neighbourhood for more than a year, police said.

'This is outrageous. The killers of an innocent child should be awarded exemplary punishment. The government needs to back up this case so that the culprits could not get scot-free,' a human rights activist called Sheryar Rizwan told the Press Trust of India.

Pakistan's child labour problem

Pakistan has huge numbers of children at work, and according to a 2018 report by the Human Rights Commission of Pakistan (HRCP) some 12 million are employed.

The abuse of young domestic staff has made the news before.

Two years ago, an eight-year-old child maid was allegedly beaten to death by her employers for releasing their prized parrots from a cage.

Zohra Shah opened the cage to feed the birds, only for the birds to fly away. Her enraged employers at the home in Rawalpindi, near Islamabad, were accused of beating her unconscious before dumping her at a nearby hospital. She died of her injuries.

In another notorious case, the Supreme Court set aside the extended three-year sentence against a former judge and his wife who were convicted for torturing their 10-year-old maid Tayyaba.

The United Nations last month warned that across the world, the disruption to schools caused by two years of Covid lockdowns had put more children at risk of being forced into child labour.

Some nine million more children will be at risk of being forced into work by the end of 2022, the UN's children's rights arm, Unicef, warned.

The problem of child labour is worldwide. The UN's labour wing, the International Labour Organisation, estimating a decade ago that more than 17 million children below the age of 18 were employed as maids, servants or domestic help.

The issue was again highlighted in the UK this week when Sir Mo Farah, the four-time Olympic running champion, said he had previously lied about his background as a refugee and had in fact been trafficked as a child.

Somali-born Sir Mo described in a BBC documentary how he was brought to Britain aged nine and said he was forced to cook, clean and look after younger children by a couple who told him he would never see his real family again if he told anyone the truth.

13 July 2022

Sir Mo Farah reveals he was trafficked to the UK

The true story of an Olympic legend.

Sir Mo Farah's impact on the running world has been undeniable, as a four-time Olympic champion and the holder of six World titles, there are few people in the UK who don't know his name, or his infamous 'Mobot' celebration. Originally from Somaliland, Farah has told people throughout his career that he came to the UK from Somalia with his parents as a refugee, however, he has now revealed that he was in fact trafficked to the UK illegally and forced to work as a domestic servant as a child.

The revelation comes as Farah explains he is ready to tell the truth about his childhood experience, which he shares in full in his upcoming BBC documentary, The Real Mo Farah.

In the documentary, the Olympic legend shares: 'Most people know me as Mo Farah but it's not my name or it's not the reality. The real story is I was born in Somaliland, north of Somalia, as Hussein Abdi Kahin.

'Despite what I've said in the past, my parents never lived in the UK.

'When I was four my dad was killed in the civil war, as a family, we were torn apart. I was separated from my mother, and I was brought into the UK illegally under the name of another child called Mohamed Farah.'

The story of Hussein Abdi Kahin

When only four years old, Hussein Abdi Kahin's father, Abdi, was killed by stray gunfire during civil violence in Somaliland. After this, his family was torn apart, and when he was eight or nine years old, he was taken from Somaliland to neighbouring Djibouti to stay with family. He didn't stay in Djibouti for long and was flown to the UK by a woman he didn't know, who claimed she'd be taking him to Europe to live with his relatives there. He was, as most children growing up in a war-torn country would have been, excited at the chance of a fresh start.

However, that excitement was quickly diminished after landing in the UK. The woman told him to tell people his name was Mohamed, giving him fake travel documents with his photograph next to another child's name. When in the flat in Hounslow that Hussein would spend the next years of his life in, the woman took the piece of paper he had with his relatives' contact details on and tore it apart, throwing it away, it's at this moment he revealed he knew he was in trouble.

This woman then forced Hussein to work as a domestic servant, telling him he would do as he was told if he ever wanted to see his family again. For the first few years of his life in the UK, this was all Hussein knew, but when he turned 12, he enrolled in the local Community College, a turning point in his life.

Teachers here could see that something was wrong, but in PE class Hussein thrived, gaining enough confidence to

open up to his PE teacher Mr Watkinson about his true past and identity, and the horrible situation he found himself in. Because of this confession, social services managed to intervene, and Hussein was fostered by the mother of one of his friends, another Somali family.

His love for sport continued and his running prowess soon shone. So that he was able to compete in competitions outside of the UK, Mr Watkinson helped him apply for British citizenship under the name 'Mohamed Farah', which was granted in July 2000.

He then went on to become the champion runner we know him as, with the country shouting a name that he wasn't born with whenever he raced. In fact, he was so affected by his past that it took him years to reveal to his wife, Tania Farah, the truth of his childhood.

His upcoming documentary allows Hussein to share the truth of his story, and he hopes it'll reframe public perspective on trafficking and slavery. In the documentary, we see him connect with his family, talk about his experience and even meet with the real Mohamed Farah whose identity he was given when he came to the UK.

The fight against child trafficking

It can be easy to think of child trafficking as a problem that doesn't affect the UK, but with the news of one of the country's most beloved athletes' traumatic childhood experience, it brings the issue much closer to home for many people.

The reasons for child trafficking can be wide, from domestic labour like in the case of Farah to recruitment for armed groups, sex work and even adoption. In fact, Farah's story is quite typical, as two situations when children are most likely to be trafficked is after their family is torn apart by natural disasters or violent conflict, as was happening in Somaliland at the time.

Child trafficking is a lucrative business for those involved, and it's estimated to be a $150 billion a year industry. Even for those like Farah who manage to escape and find a safer home, reintegrating can be challenging, and people can be left with lasting emotional and physical trauma, as well as missing out or having their education delayed.

Trafficking is a complex issue that requires working in partnership with government, communities and children themselves to solve. At World Vision, our work aims to tackle the root causes of trafficking through a combination of different approaches, ranging from prevention and protection to prosecution and advocacy work.

By supporting children and their communities in areas where the risks are high, we can identify potential victims and report signs of trafficking, advocate for children's rights, provide the things they need such as emergency shelter and essential care to keep families together, and help stop child trafficking. As well as that, we're always on hand to provide education about the rights of victims of trafficking, including the rights of those who are trafficked to the UK.

We are also part of the PACE (Partnership Against Child Exploitation), a partnership of organisations that are working together to combat the exploitation of children in the worst forms of child labour, including domestic labour like Farah faced when first arriving in the UK.

The battle against child trafficking is far from over, but we hope that by Sir Mo Farah sharing his story, more people will look for ways to help support UK charities like ours who are working with communities to end the practice.

We have to remember that, although Farah's story has a happy ending, many children's do not, and we need to continue working tirelessly to fight child trafficking.

12 July 2022

A child should go to school, not to work

Domboué Nibéissé is 15 years old and enjoys being back at school after having spent several years working in cotton fields in Burkina Faso.

By Domboué Nibéissé

My name is Domboué Nibéissé. I am 15 years old. When I was 9 years old I had to leave school to work in the cotton fields.

I live with my aunt, I have five older brothers, five older sisters and three younger sisters.

I started school when I was 8 years old, but one year later in CE1 (2nd year of primary school) I stopped school because we didn't have enough money. I was upset not to go. I didn't like it because my friends would go to school and leave me on my own.

When I stopped going to school, I went to work in the fields to earn some money. It was difficult work and tiring. We picked cotton by hand. There were a few other children working alongside me.

I used to work in cotton fields like this all day long. I used to start sowing at 9am, rest around 1pm, and at 4pm I would go home. I was given between 500 (USD 0.79) and 750 francs (USD 1.19).

When it was not sowing or harvest time, on market days, I helped sell clothes to make some money.

When I was 11 years old, a school reintegration centre (Centre de Stratégie de Scolarisation Accélérée / Passerelle - SSA/P) contacted us so that I could return to school. I was able to join the centre, and I was really happy because I knew I would learn a lot.

At the SSA/P centre, I learned to count and read in Dioula, we did our homework in Dioula, and then we learned to count and do calculations and homework in French. Thanks to this, I was able to go back to school in the formal system, in CM1 class (fourth year of primary school).

Now that I am back at school I feel good. I am very happy because I have found my friends. During recess I like to play football with them.

My favourite subject is the study of texts. When I grow up I want to be a policeman.

Children belong in school, not at work. When I was working I didn't like it because it made me tired. And even though school is sometimes a bit difficult, I will learn and one day I will earn a living from it.

Fast facts

- 160 million children aged 5 to 17 work worldwide.
- 70% of the world's child labour is in agriculture. Cotton is one of the most common commodities produced using child and forced labour.
- The CLEAR Cotton project contributes to national efforts to eliminate child labour in the cotton, textile and garment value chain in Burkina Faso, Mali, Pakistan and Peru.
- In Burkina Faso, CLEAR Cotton has set up a school reintegration programme: the Stratégie de Scolarisation Accélérée - Passerelle (SSA/P).
- The project is co-funded by the European Union (EU) and the International Labour Organization (ILO), and is implemented by the ILO in collaboration with the Food and Agriculture Organization (FAO).

16 May 2022

World Day Against Child Labour 2022

All you need to know about history, significance and theme.

Several campaigns and seminars around the topic are organised on this day. The events aims to bring forward solutions to combat the global menace and ensure that children the world over have a happy and healthy life.

World Day Against Child Labour is marked every year on 12 June. The day aims to raise awareness about the exploitation of children who are engaged in child labour. Children are classified as child labourers when they are either too young to work, or they are made to take part in hazardous activities that may have an impact on their physical, social, mental or educational development.

The day also focuses on what more needs to be done to eliminate this practice. It aims to bring together governments and civil society organisations to combat child labour.

History:

The International Labour Organization (ILO) started observing World Day Against Child Labour in 2002 with an aim to highlight the plight of children who are the victims of child labour. The day serves as a catalyst to take forward the global movement against the practice. The ILO Convention No. 182, which deals with the worst forms of child labour, as well as ILO Convention No. 138, that deals with the minimum age for employment, are the two main global conventions on the issue.

What is the theme for this year?

The theme for this year is 'Universal Social Protection to End Child Labour'. The theme of the day focuses on increased investment in social protection schemes and systems to develop solid social protection mechanisms for protection from child labour.

While significant advancement has been made in the reduction of child labour over the last two decades, the pace has slowed down over time, or even paused, like during the period 2016-2020. A total of 160 million children are still engaged in child labour, with some of them as young as five years old.

Significance:

The World Day Against Child Labour gives an opportunity to gain further support of individual governments as well as civil society, social partners and others in the campaign against child labour.

According to the United Nations, one in 10 children aged five years and over, were involved in child labour worldwide at the beginning of 2020 – which is equal to an estimated 160 million children, or 97 million boys and 63 million girls. Africa has the biggest share of child labourers – 72 million.

Several campaigns and seminars around the topic are organised on this day. The events aim to bring forward solutions to combat the global menace and ensure that children the world over have a happy and healthy life.

12 June 2022

'Kidfluencers' are being exploited and more needs to be done to protect them

MPs are questioning the absence of protection for 'kidfluencers' – children who are influencers – against exploitation.

By Anugraha Sundaravelu

A report from the UK's Digital, Culture, Media and Sport (DCMS) Committee highlighted the rapid expansion in influencer culture which has exposed regulatory gaps which leave children at risk of exploitation and unacceptable compliance with advertising rules.

In their recommendations, MPs say children, parents and schools must be given more support in developing media literacy and for rules around advertising for children to be bolstered. It also calls for a code of conduct for influencer marketing to be commissioned.

With the child influencer market booming, children featuring in online content across social media platforms are earning income through sponsorship and partnerships with brands on accounts managed by their parents.

To protect these children the report calls for updates to UK child labour regulations to reflect the growth of child influencers.

In addition, the report urges the government to conduct a study into the influencer ecosystem so it can be properly regulated as it grows as well as manage rules around pay standards and practice, and advertising regulators be given more power to enforce the law around advertising and close influencer loopholes.

'The rise of influencer culture online has brought significant new opportunities for those working in the creative industries and a boost to the UK economy,' said Julian Knight, the chair of the committee.

'However, as is so often the case where social media is involved, if you dig below the shiny surface of what you see on screen you will discover an altogether murkier world where both the influencers and their followers are at risk of exploitation and harm online.'

Child viewers, who are still developing digital literacy, are in particular danger in an environment where not everything is always as it seems, while there is a woeful lack of protection for young influencers who often spend long hours producing financially lucrative content at the direction of others.'

Knight added that 'inaction' had left regulations behind the times in a digital world, and that was particularly concerning when it came to the protection of children.

Influencer content on social media is becoming an increasingly popular media genre for children, particularly on YouTube. According to Ofcom, in 2021 up to half of children said they watched vloggers or YouTube influencers.

The committee's report said it had heard concerns during its inquiry that some children within the influencer economy were being used by parents and family members – who often manage their online accounts – who were seeking to capitalise on the lucrative online market.

Concerns were also raised about how content featuring children can also affect their privacy and bring security risks. The reports asked for new legislation with provisions on working hours and conditions for child influencers, protection of the child's earnings, ensure a right to erasure, and bring the child's labour arrangements under the oversight of local authorities.

What is Ofcom and what does it cover?

Ofcom is the regulator for the communications services that we use and rely on each day.

The watchdog makes sure people get the best from their broadband, home phone and mobile services, as well as keeping an eye on TV and radio.

Ofcom deals with most content on television, radio and video-on-demand services, including the BBC. However, if your complaint is about something you saw or heard in a BBC programme, you may need to complain to the BBC first.

Its rules for television and radio programmes are set out in the Broadcasting Code. The rules in the Broadcasting Code also apply to the BBC iPlayer.

This Broadcasting Code is the rule book that broadcasters have to follow and it covers a number of areas, including; protecting the under-18s, protecting audiences from harmful and/or offensive material and ensuring that news, in whatever form, is reported with due accuracy and presented with due impartiality.

Audiences can complain to Ofcom if they believe a breach of the Broadcasting Code has been made.

Every time Ofcom receives a complaint from a viewer or listener, they assess it to see if it needs further investigation.

If Ofcom decide to investigate, they will include the case in a list of new investigations, published in the Broadcast and On Demand Bulletin.

An investigation is a formal process which can take some time depending on the complexity of the issues involved.

Ofcom can also launch investigations in the absence of a complaint from a viewer or listener.

9 May 2022

Recurring infringements of children's rights

In past ages, children were their parents' property and not considered persons of their own. That changed in the 20th century.

By Sabine Balk

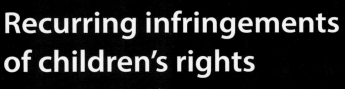

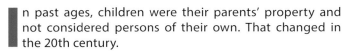

In past ages, children were their parents' property and not considered persons of their own. That changed in the 20th century.

Modern society considers children to be individuals who enjoy personal rights. These are universal principles which the UN General Assembly adopted in 1989 when it passed the Convention on the Rights of the Child. All member nations ratified it, with one exception: the USA. The Convention is the most important human-rights document in regard to children. Girls and boys are entitled to health services, an education, social inclusion and a say in everything that concerns them. They must be free to develop their own personality.

To what extent children's rights are actually respected, is another matter. Things diverge from country to country. Among other things, it depends on how well the rule of law is enforced. It is a huge challenge that infringements of children's rights often have no legal repercussions, even when those infringements are evident.

It is striking that breaches of children's rights are systematically correlated with poverty. That is true in countries with low and high incomes. In many developing countries, poor families depend on the money their children earn doing hard physical work. Poverty also leads to traumatic premature marriages, forced prostitution and enslavement of children. Far too often, parents' income does not suffice to properly feed and take care of all daughters and sons. They have no choice but to 'marry off' daughters and traffic children into enslavement.

Because of their families' poverty, many children do not get a formal education. Their parents simply cannot afford to send them to school and make them work instead. Under age refugees struggle in particular. Their rights are seriously breached in many ways.

Even in prosperous nations like Germany, infringements occur regularly. The welfare benefits poor families receive, for example, do not suffice for a balanced and nutritious diet. Moreover, German schools are known to do a systematically poor job of educating children of immigrants. A network of 100 organisations is committed to the full implementation of the UN Convention on the Rights of the Child in Germany. They report that educational opportunities are worse for children from disadvantaged families. The same kids also experience violence and discrimination more often. Their lives are marked by physical wounds and mental trauma long-term.

Experts say that it is not enough to sign up to the UN Convention. Many nations have enshrined children's rights in their constitutions, since adopting the rights in national law facilitates enforcement. It must be possible to take culprits to court. Germany is a laggard in this regard too and has not spelled out children's rights in its constitution in spite of repeated admonitions by the UN.

Regrettably, minors around the world are largely excluded from political life. In most countries, the voting age is 18, though some nations have lowered it to 16 – Austria, for example, and some Latin American countries. Younger kids, however, are denied representation. Governments and legislators must therefore foster serious exchange with children and teenagers. Policymakers must consider the interests of the youngest people – that is especially true in our era of fast escalating climate crisis.

28 September 2021

UK youth justice system risks breaching children's rights, says UNICEF UK

UNICEF UK raises serious concerns over children's human rights within the UK youth justice system.

A new report from UNICEF UK finds that the UK youth justice system is failing children and risks breaching their human rights. Key areas for concern identified within the report include the over representation of children from Black, Asian and Minority Ethnic (BAME) backgrounds within the youth justice system, unsatisfactory conditions within youth detention, the widespread use of in-humane practices such as solitary confinement, tasers, and spit-hoods, and the low ages of criminal responsibility across all four UK nations.

The report finds:

♦ In the year ending March 2019, in England and Wales, Black children were over 4 times more likely to be arrested than white children.[1]

♦ Data gathered from 29 police forces reveals that 51% of children who had tasers used on them in England were from a BAME background. [2]

♦ In the year ending March 2019, in England and Wales, the proportion of Black children given a caution, or a sentence was nearly 3 times higher than the proportion of Black children in the 10-17 population.[3]

♦ In 2017 HM Chief Inspector of Prisons said: 'There was not a single establishment that we inspected in England and Wales in which it was safe to hold children and young people.'[4]

The four UK nations also have some of the lowest ages of criminal responsibility in the world, where children as young as 10 in England, Wales and Northern Ireland can be charged with a criminal offence and processed within the criminal justice system. Scotland recently voted to increase their age of criminal responsibility from eight years to 12 years old – but this is still below the UN recommendation of at least 14 years old.

Anna Kettley, Deputy Executive Director of Programmes and Advocacy at UNICEF UK, said:

'Children who come into contact with the law are some of the most vulnerable and marginalised in society, often they have been in the care system, experienced neglect or abuse and may have been excluded from school.

'Our report finds that the youth justice system is failing in its duty to protect and uphold children's human rights – to keep them safe and protect them from harm. We need a system that upholds their rights and gives every child who comes into contact with the law the opportunity to positively turn their life around.

The new report *'A Rights-Based Analysis of Youth Justice in the United Kingdom'* is UNICEF UK's first in-depth look into the UK youth justice system, and reviews, from a child rights perspective, the contexts in which youth justice functions in each of the four UK nations. Whilst it finds that positive steps, like the significant reduction in the number of child arrests and children within the system, as well as the creation of 'Outcome 21' which reduces the criminalisation of children for sexting offences, have been made, there remain significant areas which do not meet international children's rights standards. The report includes 45 recommendations for the UK government and devolved administrations to consider which include:

♦ Raising the minimum age of criminal responsibility to at least 14 years of age

♦ Stopping the use of in-humane practices on children such as solitary confinement, tasers and spit-hoods

♦ Committing to ensuring the anonymity of children who come into contact with the law and appear at court

♦ Investing in research to better understand the true impact of diversion and how it relates to girls, BAME, school-excluded and care-experienced children

To mark the release of the report, UNICEF UK will be holding two online panel sessions – one relating to England and Wales and the other to Scotland and Northern Ireland, which will bring together key stakeholders from civil society, academia and practice to discuss the key findings to emerge from the report.

8 December 2020

1. Ministry of Justice and Youth Justice Board (2020). Youth Justice Statistics 2018 to 2019. London: Ministry of Justice and Youth Justice Board. p.6
2. CRAE (2019). State of Children's Rights in England 2018. Policing and Criminal Justice. London: Children's Rights Alliance for England.
3. Ministry of Justice and Youth Justice Board (2020). Youth Justice Statistics: 2018 to 2019. London: Ministry of Justice and Youth Justice Board. p.16
4. HM Chief Inspector of Prisons (2017). Annual Report 2016-17. London: HMCIP p.9

Government's refusal to provide care to every child looked after by the state shames Britain

Ministers have failed to see that an absence of care and nurturing lies at the heart of harms to children, says Carolyne Willow.

By Carolyne Willow

On this day, 30 years ago, the UK Government made a pledge to the United Nations that it would honour the Convention on the Rights of the Child, an international human rights treaty containing comprehensive state obligations towards children.

Who could have anticipated that today we would be challenging the Government of the world's sixth-richest nation on its refusal to provide care to every child in its care?

The Office for National Statistics reports that 60% of 22 year olds in the UK still live with their parents. Yet, a third of children in care aged 16 and 17 live in properties where there are no adult carers. The Government is regulating to make the absence of care legitimate and acceptable.

When it is not in their best interests to live with members of their family, or with foster carers or in an establishment registered as a children's home (which includes many boarding and residential schools), since September this year the law provides that children must live in settings where they receive care and supervision (a list of permissible places is specified).

However, this only applies to children who are aged 15 years or younger. A legal dividing line has been forged. On one side are children who must always receive care; on the other, are those who can go without.

My small charity, Article 39, is taking the Government to court over this discriminatory treatment of 16 and 17 year olds. As well as age-based age discrimination, boys and children from black, Asian and ethnic minority communities are disproportionately placed in non-care settings. The High Court hearing is scheduled for next February.

It is true that non-care settings have been used for children in care for many decades, certainly pre-dating the UK's promise to provide special protection and assistance to children separated from their families in line with article 20 of the Convention on the Rights of the Child. However, numbers have spiralled over the past decade and there is an abundance of evidence of very serious harms – violence from within and outside the properties, children with serious mental health difficulties struggling alone, high rates of children running away and going missing, and children feeling abandoned and desperate.

Twenty-two children in care aged 16 and 17 died while living in properties without care between 2018 and 2020. Article 39's own research shows that 64 councils were notified of 334 allegations against adults working in non-care settings in the three years to March 2021.

In May 2019, BBC's Newsnight reported the case of a child moved from foster care into supported accommodation at 16, who said: 'I felt very alone for quite a while. I just felt like I was dumped into this place, and I didn't really know what to do.' When asked whether an ordinary parent would move a 16-year-old child into this environment, she replied: 'Not at all, not at all, there's a massive safety risk behind it... it's just a massive shock really.'

During a discussion with care leavers, held as part of the Government's consultation on changing the law, one young man told me that he had been the victim of a very serious crime by a member of staff at his 'supported' accommodation (where he lived between the ages of 16 and 18). He only found help after he went back to his old children's home to speak with the manager there.

Ministers have failed to see that it is the absence of loving care and nurturing which lies at the heart of harms to children.

The Education Secretary at the time of the legal change, Gavin Williamson, said that he could not imagine any child under the age of 16 living in a place where they don't receive care. Presumably, the minister then in charge of the

country's education system was able to visualise the plight of children in care aged 16 and 17 studying for GCSE and 'A' Level exams while living in accommodation alongside adults trying to cope with addiction, mental health problems and having recently left prison.

Social worker Rebekah Pierre recently published extracts from the diary she wrote as a highly vulnerable teenager in care. In it, she observed that she was 'intimidated by the angry mob outside the entrance, leering, laughing. The loneliness is astounding; if I needed help I could shout no one'.

Yesterday, the Department for Education signalled its plan to press on with regulating the absence of care in these buildings. As well as giving the green light to an inferior inspection process – whereby only a sample of providers' properties will be inspected instead of every place where children live – the Government unashamedly announced that it has 'no intention of banning the mixing of different age groups'.

When the UK ratified the Convention on the Rights of the Child, two groups of children were deliberately excluded: child refugees and children in prison. It took until November 2008 for the UK's reservations on protection for child refugees and keeping children out of adult prisons to be formally lifted.

Yet, here we are in 2021 with unaccompanied children – including those who have survived treacherous Channel crossings on flimsy boats – more than six times more likely to be put into accommodation where they don't receive any care. And it's acknowledged in Government papers, released through a Freedom of Information request, that the very

significant increase in children entering care as teenagers is connected to the marked reduction in child imprisonment.

The Child Safeguarding Practice Review Panel – recently given the task of reviewing the circumstances of the appalling death of little Arthur Labinjo-Hughes – reported this year that 'children were coming into care in adolescence having experienced long-term parental abuse and neglect'. But the child welfare system has not opened its arms to teenagers with high levels of need that in the past may have been hidden out of sight in our child prisons.

Instead, it has recalibrated and built an annex to the care system for those it deems able to manage without care – with 39% of children living in 'semi-independent' accommodation having been put there within less than a week of entering care. Like those languishing in child prisons, these are disproportionately black boys.

Paradoxically, while the prisons inspectorate has care as one of its five categories of expectations for child prisons, when inspectors start their selective inspections of supported accommodation for teenagers in care, expected in 2023, Ofsted won't be checking that children are cared for. The absurdity of this could only be matched by hospitals without nurses, schools without teachers, and swimming pools without lifeguards.

16 December 2021

Carolyne Willow is the director of the charity Article 39

Calls to ban smacking in England as children are 'more vulnerable than adults'

England should follow the lead of Scotland and Wales by banning smacking, the children's commissioner has said.

By James Hockaday

Dame Rachel de Souza is calling for a change of the law, but some within the Government fear criminalising parents would be a nanny-state policy.

She told Times Radio: 'I absolutely abhor, and I'm against, violence of any kind against children.

'Because children are more vulnerable than adults, I think we do need to ensure that their rights are supported.'

Last month Wales made any type of corporal punishment, including smacking, hitting, slapping and shaking, illegal in the country.

The ban marks the end of the common law defence of 'reasonable punishment' for naughty behaviour.

Parents or anyone who is responsible for a child while the parents are absent can now face criminal or civil charges if they are found to have physically disciplined a young person in any way.

Critics of the law change have said it will criminalise parents, but the Welsh Government insisted the move was about protecting children's rights. It followed a ban in Scotland in 2020.

At the moment, parents smacking their children is still allowed in England and Northern Ireland as long as it constitutes 'reasonable punishment' under the law.

Whether the defence was accepted depends on the circumstances of each case, taking into consideration factors such as the age of the child and the nature of the contact, including whether it left a red mark or was carried out with a fist or implement such as a cane or belt.

Dame Rachel urged ministers to look at how the legislation moved through the Welsh assembly and said she would support a decision to follow suit.

'I think we've got a great opportunity to look, watch it, as it's embedded (in Wales), and I would be supportive – certainly, from what I've seen so far – I would be supportive if our government decided to do the same,' she said.

Although Dame Rachel acknowledged that 'protections' for children are already 'enshrined in law' in England, she still thought more change was neeeded.

'I certainly admire Scotland and Wales moving on this. It's certainly something that I think we should consider,' she added.

However, a government source said there were no plans to change the law, the Times reports.

'Most people would say a light smack on the arm from a parent to a child isn't child abuse,' they said.

'We trust parents to discipline their children, when necessary, in the way they think is right.

'We've purposely not interfered in that too much. Child abuse is an entirely separate matter.'

Labour leader Sir Keir Starmer previously said the move should be mirrored in England and Northern Ireland, calling it 'the right thing' to do.

A survey commissioned by the National Society for the Prevention of Cruelty to Children found more than two-thirds of adults in England believe it is wrong for parents or carers to physically punish their child, with 58% thinking it was already illegal.

More than 60 nations worldwide have legislated against the physical punishment of children.

Today in the Commons, Conservative chairman of the Education Select Committee Robert Halfon called for a debate on whether parents should be permitted to smack their children.

The MP for Harlow said: 'If I walked down to the frontbench and smacked the Leader of the House I would be possibly done for assault, if I smacked a dog I would be possibly done for cruelty to that dog.

'Yet, when we talk about the smacking of children, we say that it's a nanny state if we question this – even though we tell parents they must put seatbelts in the back of cars for children's safety.'

While he did not call for an 'outright ban' on smacking children, Halfon said he thought the Children's Commissioner was 'courageous and right' to raise the issue.

Commons Leader Mark Spencer said parents 'have the right to chastise their children in a way in which they see fit'.

He replied: 'I think it is something which is worthy of debate, I think colleagues across the House would want to engage with that debate. I will say on a personal level, I do think that parents have the right to chastise their children in a way in which they see fit.

'But there clearly is a line where that stretches over into abuse. You know, the authorities are very robust in making sure children are safe in the United Kingdom. But it is something which is worthy of debate and I would encourage him to apply for an adjournment debate or a backbench business debate.'

21 April 2022

Excluding children from school 'violates their moral rights'

'Some people believe that by punishing you serve a developmental good, that it teaches students that they should behave better. But it just doesn't seem to be true.'

By Neil Shaw

The use of exclusions in English schools often violates the 'moral rights' of children, according to a new report.

And schools need extra support if they're to implement 'wide, systemic reform' to ensure children are not 'disproportionately harmed' when removed from classrooms.

That's according to a new study by Dr John Tillson, Senior Lecturer in the Philosophy of Education at Liverpool Hope University, and Laura Oxley, a PhD research student in the Department of Education at the University of York.

They argue school exclusions in the UK need to move from being a routine occurrence to a measure of absolute 'last resort'.

Their paper, published in the journal Theory and Research in Education, suggests exclusions deprive children of access to adequate education while also potentially putting them in mental and physical harm's way.

Exclusions are also often an ineffective deterrent to bad behaviour and using removal from classrooms as a punishment can exacerbate feelings of rejection and isolation.

Dr Tillson and Ms Oxley instead want to see the blanket use of exclusions replaced with a 'restorative, collaborative' approach to tackling problem behaviours in classrooms.

Speaking about the research, Dr Tillson says exclusion as a 'non-punitive preventative' measure may sometimes be justified to protect others in the school community, but adds: 'There are actually very few situations in which exclusions can be morally defended as the only option available.

'It is often thought that you've got broadly protective, developmental and just-desert based reasons to penalise through exclusion.

'Some people believe that by punishing you serve a developmental good, that it teaches students that they should behave better. But it just doesn't seem to be true.

'And it seems especially not to be true when it comes to school exclusion, which comes at the end of a long line of punitive treatment which has shown itself to have failed.

'It doesn't seem to make sense as an educative vehicle. It's not an effective lesson.'

Ms Oxley adds: 'How does excluding someone from the school community help them learn the values of that community?

'It doesn't foster belonging. It creates rejection and resentment - exacerbating behaviours. The child may feel, "You've rejected me, so I will reject you".

'If a student makes an academic mistake, they typically receive lots of support to help them correct that mistake. Whereas when a child makes a behavioural mistake often the immediate response is that the child should be punished.'

Temporary and permanent exclusions - both external and 'internal', where the child is isolated from peers but still on school premises - have been increasing markedly in the UK since 2013 - and the UK has a school exclusion rate that is ten times greater than that of any other country in Europe.

It's a particular issue in England, where there were 7,900 permanent exclusions in England between 2017 and 2018, compared with just three in Scotland.

The new study considers exclusion from the point of view of the United Nations' Convention on the Rights of the Child, which the UK signed in 1990.

Questioning the notion of exclusion as a punishment, Dr Tillson explains: 'Two of the weighty interests identified in the Convention are an interest in educational opportunities, and an interest in being safe and free from harm.

'You might think that punishment can sometimes protect those things.

'If a child poses some kind of a threat to another person it might seem entirely reasonable to remove that threat.

'But that threat has to be removed at proportional costs. You can't impose excessive harms on someone through exclusion to remove only a small threat.

'And in the absence of good educational opportunities for people who are excluded or who are in alternative provision, it's even less okay to exclude them, because you do more harm to them.

'Think about the adequacy of a child's education. If keeping a child in school gives them access to adequate education and doesn't diminish anyone else's education below a threshold of adequacy, we may not have a reason to remove them, even though removing them would improve everyone else's education.

'It's about schools being mindful of disproportionate harm.'

There's also the question of how responsible a child truly is for their behaviours, according to Dr Tillson, who also wants to see an end to the stigmatisation of exclusions, which arises when the threat of being sent home is wielded as a weapon.

So why are exclusion rates soaring in England?

Dr Tillson says performance reviews are a big factor, creating a 'perverse incentive' to expel lower performing students to improve league table rankings.

Meanwhile Ms Oxley says: 'There needs to be a shift in culture in terms of how schools and headteachers think about exclusion.

'It needs to be something used in exceptional circumstances, rather than something that's just part of behavioural policy.

'A big problem is that a lot of schools feel they don't have another option. They ask, "What else can we do? This child has hit another child, this child is disrupting every class they're in? All the other schools are excluding - we need to behave in the same way".'

Reform to exclusion is also not about undermining the safety of teachers.

Ms Oxley states: 'If there's a threat to a teacher, and that teacher is at risk of being harmed, then excluding the child to ensure the teacher's safety is something that may need to be considered.

'But when you look at what exclusions are commonly used for, the most common reason, for a number of years, is due to persistently disruptive behaviour - which doesn't suggest that the child's behaviour is actually causing an immediate danger to others, as persistent disruption is something that is built up over time.

'It may be causing a disruption to the education of others, but there are other alternative education provisions that can provide education for that child in a different environment, rather than excluding them from education completely.'

Harms caused by exclusion are myriad, according to Dr Tillson and Ms Oxley.

Internal isolations are described as a lesser form of 'solitary confinement' and 'social deprivation' with obvious ramifications for the child's mental health.

Ms Oxley says: 'We have to ask, what is the aim of that punishment? What is the child supposed to learn from that experience, and is there another way for the child to be taught this lesson that's more effective?

'Some schools show good practice with their use of internal isolations and use the time to undertake restorative work. This is far more constructive than having a child sit on their own, completing worksheets.'

Children externally excluded often run the risk of being groomed into gangs or being recruited into county lines drug running, says Dr Tillson.

When it comes to real change, he acknowledges that only Government led directives will give the schools the funding and resources needed to implement alternatives to exclusion.

But he adds: 'Exclusion isn't the only way we can tell a school community that a child's actions were wrong.

'If there's a restorative conversation had with that child, then the rest of the students see the response and see the child's behaviour is not being ignored.

'Headteachers and boards of governors can reconsider what the legitimate functions of exclusion are and whether or not they think a particular case does meet the threshold of not visiting disproportionate harm on an individual when they're not fully responsible for their actions.

'More resources could be poured into schools to improve the education opportunities for those in internal exclusion, or to have a higher staff to student ratio, or more dedicated staff who can think about developing strategies with particular groups of students who have trouble controlling their behaviour.

'Schools don't have these resources right now. It could take years.

'But in terms of assessing priorities and decision making frameworks, it's something that could almost happen overnight.'

The Covid-19 pandemic could also mean there's never been a more important time to assess school exclusions.

Ms Oxley states: 'We've been through a national trauma. Lives have been thrown upside down. Children may have experienced bereavements.

'There will be children who will act out their anxieties through their behaviour when they return to school. And it could result in exclusions among children who might not have been at risk of being excluded before the pandemic.

'Again, we have to ask what we actually gain from exclusions? If a child is anxious about going to school and you send them home in response to that, it's not solving the problem.

'They're still going to be anxious about going to school.'

The research was funded by the Center for Ethics and Education, and is part of a wider 'Pedagogies of Punishment' project led by Dr Tillson and Dr Winston C Thompson, of The Ohio State University, USA.

22 June 2020

Why is child marriage legal in the West?

It's the one type of slavery the West ignores.

By Ayaan Hirst Ali

New York Officially Bans Child Marriage, only Sixth State in the U.S. to do so.' You might picture this headline on a yellowing newspaper in the archives of a public library. But in actual fact it appeared online, less than a month ago. And yes, you read it correctly. New York is only the sixth American state to ban child marriage, meaning there is still a legal pathway to marrying a minor in 44 states.

Child marriage is merely a subset of the wider problem of forced marriage, which is staggering in scale. In 2016, the International Labour Organization found that '15.4 million people were living in a forced marriage to which they had not consented'. 37% of those victims are under the age of 18, and 44% of those children were 'forced to marry before the age of 15 years'. 'While men and boys,' the report states, 'can also be victims of forced marriage,' 88% of victims are female. That figure rises among child victims of forced marriage: 96% were girls.

For me, the subject of forced marriage is personal. When I was living in Kenya, my father arranged for me to marry a man I had never met. His name was Osman Moussa. He was 27. When we were introduced, only six days before the marriage, I found that he was bald, dim and expected me to give him six sons.

Before the nikah ceremony, which would legally wed us, I begged my father to reconsider. I had no interest in the man he had chosen for me and dreaded a lifetime with him. My father insisted and when I continued to resist, he reminded me of my place. In the end, my father married me to Osman when I wasn't even there – which might have been an issue had my participation been a matter of concern. But the arrangement was a mere transfer of ownership from one man to the next; my presence, let alone my consent, was not required.

Fortunately for me, I was not a child when this happened. I was 22 and had the self-confidence to flee to the Netherlands to escape my future with Osman. What if I had been 15, without the wherewithal or determination to flee?

But while my story might sound exotic, forced marriages and child marriages do not occur only in far-away countries. They are happening in the West today. This April, Unchained At Last, an organisation fighting child and forced marriages in the United States, released a study that found 'nearly 300,000 minors, under the age of 18, were legally married in the US between 2000 and 2018'. The victims' religious and ethnic backgrounds varied, but the vast majority were girls. Some were as young as 10.

In the United Kingdom, the situation is hardly any better. Here, child marriage is 'thriving'; according to official data, between 2008 and 2017 more than 2,740 minors were married in England and Wales – a disturbing figure which doesn't include minors wed in traditional ceremonies or taken abroad for the ceremony. Karma Nirvana, a British charity, recently reported 'it had seen a 150% increase in teenagers calling about forced marriage since lockdowns began on March 23'. They expect that figure to rise now that the UK has removed most of its Covid-19 restrictions and gatherings are allowed to take place.

It's encouraging, then, that UK introduced a bill this year that would close the child marriage loophole, which allows 16 and 17-year-olds to marry, with their parents' permission. Health Secretary Sajid Javid, for what it's worth, has committed his support, stating that 'child marriage is child abuse'. Meanwhile, several states in the US are also fighting to end this practice within their borders; eleven states introduced legislation this year that would ban all marriages for those under 18. (New York and Rhode Island have already succeeded.)

All this has caused me to reflect on my own experiences and the countless stories I've heard from women and girls who have come to my Foundation seeking to escape or prevent a forced marriage. But at the heart of each of their tragic stories lies a simple question: what constitutes a marriage?

These days, in much of the Western world, it is a legal union of two human beings in pursuit of love, companionship and personal fulfilment. It is an agreement into which both parties willingly enter and from which they may leave if the relationship breaks down. The word 'marriage' conjures up ideas of romance, love, desire, but also of partnership, posterity and security.

But for those legally locked in marriages they didn't want, the word has a very different meaning. Fraidy Reiss, the founder of Unchained At Last, was forced into a marriage in 1995 when she was 19 years old. It quickly turned abusive. She came from an ultra-Orthodox Jewish community and eventually escaped her abuser, which led her family to shun her. When I asked her about it, she told me: 'The day I was forced into my so-called marriage to a stranger, I lost all sexual, reproductive and financial rights. My family handed me over to the stranger for a lifetime of rape, forced motherhood and domestic servitude. What part of that sounds like a "marriage"?'

Naila Amin was forced into a marriage with her 28-year-old cousin when she was just 15-years-old. Her parents brought her from New York to Pakistan for the ceremony and left her there. With the help of the US State Department, she was able to escape about five months later.

'I can only explain my marriage as a gun to my head,' she told me. 'I literally had no choice but to be married or die as a result. I was a prisoner in my own body. Even though it belonged to me, it wasn't mine.'

My friend Yasmine Mohammed escaped a forced marriage to an al-Qaeda terrorist in Canada. I recently asked her on my podcast how she viewed her relationship. Did it really constitute a marriage?

'Absolutely not. The reason is because I don't constitute a human being, so I am a thing. I am a possession that is owned by my family and I am given to him for him to now own.'

Humans beings – often young girls – treated as property. Individuals unable to leave a situation on their own accord. These descriptions call to mind another institution which also dates back to ancient times: slavery. From antiquity onwards, countless civilisations have been built upon slavery. And it still exists in many forms today, including in these so-called marriages.

Because when an adult man – whether he is in his 20s or 50s – marries an 11-year-old girl, she inevitably gains all the essential attributes of a slave: she has no real power to leave – unless she accepts total destitution, permanent ostracism, or even honour violence. She is subject to the arbitrariness and capriciousness of an authority with absolute power over her life: her husband. And she is profoundly vulnerable to physical, sexual or emotional abuse.

Behind these forced marriages lie any number of dark motives. Girls may be trafficked, perhaps after false employment promises made to families living in dire poverty, perhaps after being kidnapped. Sometimes, a girl is married to satisfy a debt. Sometimes, a girl is married to solidify a certain tribal alliance. Sometimes, a girl is married to protect a family's honour.

Sometimes, a girl is forced to marry the man who raped her because no one else will marry such a 'tainted' girl. I've seen first-hand how families pressure women and girls into marriage. There are many possible motives, but the manipulation – and the absence of true consent – is a constant.

In cases of forced marriage, particularly where honour plays a cultural role, extreme coercion can be brought to bear to ensure compliance by one or both parties. It is true that men can also be the victims of honour violence (particularly as it

pertains to sexual minorities), but in general women are the more common victims: they're generally seen as embodying the sexual honour of their tribe and community through their perceived sexual purity. Hence the need to marry them off quickly and quietly.

'Marriage' is, of course, a misnomer for these horrific situations. For a marriage to be an ethical union between two free parties, both persons have to make the decision without duress and through the use of reason. Preventing the formation of such marriages, like ending slavery, is an imperative of decency and humanity.

Yet, this year, headlines like 'Victory Against Child Marriage in New York State' contrast starkly with others, like this: 'Some NC lawmakers let child marriage ban stall because they or someone they know married as minors'. In North Carolina, children as young as 14 (the legal age to marry in North Carolina if a girl is pregnant) are being forced into 'marriages'.

Last month, Judy Wiegand came forward to testify for a ban of child marriages in North Carolina, recounting her own experiences of marrying in northern NC in 1996, at the age of 15. Her husband turned 18 soon after they wed and became her 'guardian'. As a minor, she was not able to 'go to medical appointments by herself, she needed [her husband's] permission to be on birth control, which he denied, and she couldn't sign for utilities, rent an apartment or get a driver's license without his approval'.

Yesterday, the NC House considered the 'SB 35' bill, which would raise the age of marriage to sixteen, with no more than a four years age difference allowed for those marrying at sixteen or seventeen. The bill passed unanimously – but despite these efforts towards progress, this bill remains inadequate. Sixteen and seventeen-year-olds are still minors and also need protection, as illustrated by Judy Wiegand's experiences above.

Indeed, it's striking that the North Carolina House passed over their own brightline bill, HB 41, which would raise the age of marriage to 18 years old, no exceptions, to instead let the focus sit on the watered down SB 35. We would not ignore a brightline bill if it were a slavery ban that was stalling in North Carolina – or any of the other 44 states where child marriage is still legal.

So perhaps what's needed here is a shift in terminology. To reflect what's truly happening when a family offers up their 12-year-old daughter to a 27-year-old distant cousin – and to stop people turning a blind eye for fear of being culturally insensitive – we need to call child marriages what they are: slavery.

11 August 2021

Ayaan Hirsi Ali is an UnHerd columnist. She is also a research fellow at Stanford University's Hoover Institution, Founder of the AHA Foundation, and host of The Ayaan Hirsi Ali Podcast. Her new book is *Prey: Immigration, Islam, and the Erosion of Women's Rights*.

Child Q:
strip-searches are a violation of human rights

Former director of education at the London borough where Child Q was humiliated said the incident reminded him of Apartheid South Africa

By Lester Holloway

The traumatic strip-search of Child Q in a Hackney school by police officers was a 'violation of human rights', a former director of education in the north-east London borough has said.

Professor Gus John said the humiliating intimate search on the 15-year-old girl reminded him of how children were treated in apartheid South Africa, and said this was an example of the creeping 'securitisation' of education with police patrolling school corridors.

It emerged today that 25 intimate searches were carried out on children in one year in Hackney, sparking fears that this is becoming a widespread practice in diverse and multicultural schools across Britain. Of those 25 strip-searches, 23 were black, and in almost all cases nothing incriminating was found.

Professor John warned that the practice of strip-searching was becoming increasingly common, along with school exclusions of black primary pupils for 'sexual assault'.

A report into the Child Q incident, which took place in December 2020, found that it had a traumatic effect, transforming her from a 'happy-go-lucky girl to a timid recluse that hardly speaks' and who now self-harms.

Teachers at the school searched Child Q's bag, blazer, scarf, and shoes after thinking they smelt cannabis, but when this search found nothing they called the police.

After four officers arrived, the child was subjected to an 'undignified, humiliating, and degrading' intimate search. No drugs were found.

Child Q told the police she was on her period but officers made her take out her sanitary product and then reinsert it, before teachers told her to go and sit an exam without asking how she was.

In a written statement to the review, Child Q said: 'Someone walked into the school, where I was supposed to feel safe, took me away from the people who were supposed to protect me and stripped me naked, while on my period.

'On the top of preparing for the most important exams of my life. I can't go a single day without wanting to scream, shout, cry or just give up.

'I feel like I'm locked in a box, and no one can see or cares that I just want to go back to feeling safe again, my box is collapsing around me, and no-one wants to help. I don't know if I'm going to feel normal again. I don't know how long it will take to repair my box. But I do know this can't happen to anyone, ever again.'

Professor John, who became the first black head of education when he was appointed to Hackney in 1989, said black children were increasingly being targeted by police who were not only being invited by teachers to deal with low-level matters, but in many cases police were being permanently stationed in schools.

He told *The Voice*: 'There is a war on black youth. We saw increased securitisation of schools after the 2011 riots following the killing of Mark Duggan, when the government ramped up all of those provisions and powers it gave schools. And now black children in schools are under siege.'

He added that the intimate search had violated seven clauses of the United Nations convention on the rights of children.

Campaigners believe the stationing of cops in schools is accelerating the criminalisation of black children as teachers effectively contract-out their responsibility to keep order to the police.

An official investigation into the Child Q case found that racism and the 'adultification' of black children were factors.

The report said: "Having considered the context of the incident, the views of those engaged in the review and the impact felt by Child Q and her family, racism (whether deliberate or not) was likely to have been an influencing factor in the decision to undertake a strip search.

'One feature believed to have a significance to the experience of Child Q is that of adultification bias. This concept is where adults perceive Black children as being older than they are.'

Professor John said this had echoes in the sexualisation of black primary school children who were being expelled for sexual assault. He is the co-founder of the Communities Empowerment Network which is dealing with the case of a four-year-old boy who was excluded after a 'you show me yours, I'll show you mine' incident.

Hackney MP Diane Abbott today wrote to a senior police officer in her borough, writing on Twitter:

'The indignities that Child Q was subjected to are not an aberration, they're part of a bigger picture of institutional racism and discrimination within policing.'

Zahra Bei, a teacher with 20 years experience, and campaigner in the organisation No More Exclusions, said that the education system was inflicting 'state violence' on black children.

She told *The Voice*: 'I see teachers acting more like prison guards and cops than educators.

'I don't want to de-centre the story of Child Q, but also we know there are many Child Q's that have been treated like this.'

Earlier today, *The Voice* revealed that 90% of teachers had not received diversity training on tackling racial bias in the classroom.

Bei campaigns against the high rates of exclusions of black children, as academy managers look to improve exam results, and lack of public accountability around those exclusions.

In a statement Det Supt Dan Rutland, of the Met's Central East Command, said: 'We recognise that the findings of the safeguarding review reflect this incident should never have happened.

'It is truly regrettable and on behalf of the Met Police I would like to apologise to the child concerned, her family and the wider community.'

Scotland Yard refused to say whether any disciplinary action had been taken against any officers involved, and said that they are waiting for the outcome of an investigation by the Independent Office of Police Complaints. The IOPC did not respond.

The investigation report found that the national Child Safeguarding Practice Review Panel tried to discourage investigators from looking into the case, writing '[we] would encourage you to think carefully about whether one is necessary as we felt that this case was not notifiable and did not meet the criteria for a [local child safeguarding practice review].' A review was carried out against this advice.

16 March 2022

Taliban's backtracking on girls' education, deeply damaging'

Following a U-turn over re-opening girls' secondary schools in Afghanistan, the UN human rights chief shared her 'profound frustration and disappointment' that six months after the Taliban seized power, high school girls have yet to return to the classroom.

The de facto authorities' failure to adhere to commitments to reopen schools for girls above the sixth grade – in spite of repeated commitments towards girls' education, including during my visit to Kabul two weeks ago – is deeply damaging for Afghanistan,' High Commissioner Michelle Bachelet said in a statement.

'The denial of education violates the human rights of women and girls'

– UN human rights chief

'Grave concern'

Although high schools were set to open their doors to girls nationwide, Taliban authorities reportedly reversed the move early on Wednesday, pending a ruling made on the uniforms they must wear.

'The denial of education violates the human rights of women and girls – beyond their equal right to education, it leaves them more exposed to violence, poverty and exploitation,' Ms. Bachelet explained.

Move jeopardizes Afghanistan's future: Guterres

The UN Secretary-General said in a statement later in the day, that he deeply regretted the Taliban's suspension of the return to school for high school girls.

'The start of the new school year has been anticipated by all students, girls and boys, and parents and families', said António Guterres. He added that the Taliban move 'despite repeated commitments, is a profound disappointment and deeply damaging for Afghanistan.

'The denial of education not only violates the equal rights of women and girls to education, it also jeopardizes the country's future in view of the tremendous contributions by Afghan women and girls.

'I urge the Taliban de facto authorities to open schools for all students without any further delay.'

Recounting conversations

Ms. Bachelet recalled her recent visit to Kabul, where women stressed to her that they wanted to speak to the Taliban themselves.

The women told her that they have 'information, solutions and the capability to help chart a way out of this economic, humanitarian and human rights crisis in Afghanistan.'

'They insisted upon the equal right to quality education at the primary, secondary and tertiary levels and were hopefully awaiting the reopening of schools today.'

Structural discrimination

As Afghan citizens suffer the impacts of multiple intersecting crises, the senior UN official described the decision as being of 'grave concern.'

'Disempowering half of Afghanistan's population is counterproductive and unjust,' Ms. Bachelet said, adding that 'structural discrimination such as this is also deeply damaging for the country's prospects of future recovery and development.'

She called on the Taliban to 'respect all girls' rights to education and to open schools for all students without discrimination or further delay'.

Shattered hopes

The Executive Director of the UN Children's Fund, Catherine Russell, also issued a statement describing the decision as 'a major setback for girls and their futures'.

'Millions of secondary-school girls around Afghanistan woke up hopeful today that they will be able to go back to school and resume their learning,' she said.

'It did not take long for their hopes to be shattered.'

According to Ms. Russell the decision meant that an entire generation of adolescent girls is being 'denied their right to an education and...robbed of the opportunity to gain the skills they need to build their futures.'

She urged the de facto authorities to honour their commitment to girls' education without any further delay and appealed to community leaders in every corner of the country to support the education of adolescent girls.

'All children deserve to be in school. This is the surest way to put the country on a surer path toward the peace and prosperity that the people of Afghanistan deserve,' said the UNICEF chief.

Decision deplored

The UN Assistance Mission in Afghanistan (UNAMA) responded to the news, by tweeting that it 'deplores today's reported announcement by the Taliban that they are further extending their indefinite ban on female students above the 6th grade being permitted to return school.'

23 March 2022

Key Facts

- Children and young people have the same general human rights as adults and also specific rights that recognize their special needs. (page 1)

- The KidsRights Index is the first and only global ranking of 182 countries worldwide that annually measures how children's rights are respected, and to what extent countries are committed to improving the rights of children. (page 4)

- The annual KidsRights Index is based on the nearly universally ratified United Nations Convention on the Rights of the Child (CRC), and provides a general overview of country performance on children's rights. (page 5)

- In The UK was in 169th place on the KidsRights Index in 2021. (page 5)

- In 2021, Iceland topped the KidsRights index. (page 5)

- The United Nations Convention on the Rights of the Child (UNCRC) acknowledges that every child has the right to life, the right to their own identity, and the right to express opinions and have them heard. (page 7)

- A study found that 34% of Generation Z (defined as those born from the mid-1990s to early 2000s) say they're permanently quitting social media, and 64% are taking a break from it. (page 9)

- The research also discovered that 41% of young people are made to feel anxious, sad or depressed by social media platforms like Facebook, Instagram and Snapchat. (page 9)

- Currently, France leads the way in legally preventing future harm to children because of their parents' online choices. Under French privacy law, anyone who publishes and distributes images of someone else without their explicit consent – including parents posting pictures of their own children – can face up to one year in prison or a fine of up to €45,000 (£38,000). (page 10)

- In many countries, girls are the first victims when children's human rights are violated and they often suffer double discrimination: for their age and for their gender. They are more discriminated against than boys, for being minors and female. (page 13)

- In the world there are 96 million illiterate girls aged between 15 and 24, compared to 57 million illiterate boys. (page 13)

- 50% of sexual assaults in the world are committed against girls less than 16 years old. (page 13)

- Pregnancy is the number one cause of death among 15 to 19-year-old girls. (page 14)

- Each year, 70,000 teenagers die in developing countries due to complications related to childbirth or pregnancy. (page 14)

- Currently, nine out of 10 children around the world are breathing toxins that exceed safe levels which can interfere with critical stages of organ development. (page 16)

- Unicef has predicted that air pollution will become the leading cause of child mortality by 2050. (page 16)

- The global estimates of child labour as reported by the ILO at the beginning of 2020 were 160 million children – 97 million boys and 63 million girls engaged in child labour. (page 18)

- According to the most recent ILO- UNICEF 2020 report on child labour, it is estimated that there 89.3 million children engaged in child labour between the ages of 5 –11 years old, 35.6 million between the ages of 12–14 and 35 million between the ages of 15–17 years (ILO, 2020). (page 19)

- It is hard to obtain exact figures on the numbers of children who have worked on the cacao farms. The International Labour Organization estimates 1.56 million in the Ivory Coast and Ghana alone. (page 22)

- Child trafficking is estimated to be a $150 billion a year industry. (page 24)

- 70% of the world's child labour is in agriculture. Cotton is one of the most common commodities produced using child and forced labour. (page 25)

- The four UK nations also have some of the lowest ages of criminal responsibility in the world, where children as young as 10 in England, Wales and Northern Ireland can be charged with a criminal offence and processed within the criminal justice system. (page 29)

- In the year ending March 2019, in England and Wales, Black children were over 4 times more likely to be arrested than white children. (page 29)

- At the moment, parents smacking their children is still allowed in England and Northern Ireland as long as it constitutes 'reasonable punishment' under the law. (page 32)

- More than 60 nations worldwide have legislated against the physical punishment of children. (including Scotland and Wales). (page 32)

- The UK has a school exclusion rate that is ten times greater than that of any other country in Europe. (page 33)

- There were 7,900 permanent exclusions in England between 2017 and 2018, compared with just three in Scotland. (page 33)

- In 2016, the International Labour Organization found that '15.4 million people were living in a forced marriage to which they had not consented'. 37% of those victims are under the age of 18, and 44% of those children were 'forced to marry before the age of 15 years'. 'While men and boys,' the report states, 'can also be victims of forced marriage,' 88% of victims are female. That figure rises among child victims of forced marriage: 96% were girls. (page 35)

Child exploitation

Child exploitation is a broad term which includes forced or dangerous labour, child trafficking and child prostitution. The term is used to refer to situations where children are abused – physically, verbally or sexually – or when they are submitted to unsatisfactory conditions as part of their forced or voluntary employment.

Child labour

There is no universally accepted definition of child labour. However, it might generally be said to be work for children that harms or exploits them some way (physically, mentally, morally or by blocking access to education). According to the United Nations, over 160 million children were involved in child labour worldwide at the beginning of 2020 – which is equal to an estimated 160 million children, some of them as young as five years old.

Child marriage

Where children, often before they have reached puberty, are given to be married – often to a person many years older.

Children's rights

The Convention on the Rights of the Child (CRC) is a human rights treaty which has changed the way that children are viewed and treated since it was established in 1989. The treaty sets out the civil, political, economic, social, health and cultural rights of children.

Child trafficking

'Trafficking' is not the same as 'people smuggling' where immigrants and asylum seekers pay people to help them enter another country illegally. Victims of trafficking are coerced or deceived by the person arranging their relocation. On arrival in the country of destination, a trafficked child is denied their human rights and forced into exploitation by the trafficker or person into whose control they are delivered.

Exploitation

Taking advantage of or using someone for selfish reasons.

Grooming

Actions that are deliberately performed in order to encourage a child to engage in sexual activity. For example, offering friendship and establishing an emotional connection, buying gifts etc.

International Labour Organisation (ILO)

The International Labour Organization is a United Nations agency. It was founded in 1919 to promote internationally recognised human and labour rights and improve labour conditions and living standards throughout the world.

Kidfluencer

Social media influencer under the age of 16.

KidsRights Index

The KidsRights Index is the first and the only global ranking that annually measures how children's rights are respected worldwide and to what extent countries are committed to improving the rights of children.

Slave labour

Slave labour means any form of slavery, sale and trafficking of persons, debt bondage, indentured servitude, serfdom, or forced compulsory labour.

United Nations Convention on the Rights of the Child (UNCRC)

An international human rights treaty that protects the rights of all children and young people under 18. The UK signed the convention on 19 April 1990 and ratified it on 16 December 1991. When a country ratifies the convention it agrees to do everything it can to implement it. Every country in the world has signed the convention except the USA and Somalia.

Activities

Brainstorming

♦ In small groups brainstorm what you know about children's rights.

- Compile a list of the rights you can think of, off the top of your head, as described in The United Nations Convention on the Rights of the Child (UNCRC).

- What is child labour? Name the sectors where exploitation of child labour is rife.

- Write a list of any products, brands or companies you are aware of who have been called out for their use of child labour.

- What are the most prevalent violations of children's rights in the world today?

♦ In pairs think about recent news events. Can you identify any major news stories where an infringement of a child's rights has taken place? Write a short piece describing what happened and which rights were breached.

Research

♦ In pairs, do some research into child labour in the following sectors

- agriculture

- fashion industry

- mining

- domestic work

♦ What are the risks and effects the children who work in these sectors face every day? Write up a summary of your findings and share with your class.

♦ Do some research into child marriage. In which countries is it legal? You should consider the reasons why this happens and look at the age and gender of the children involved. Produce an infograph to show your findings.

♦ Using this book and the internet, research the issue of children's right to privacy in the digital age. Is it something that concerns you? If so, in what way?

Design

♦ Choose one of the articles in this book and create an illustration to accompany it that highlights its key messages.

♦ Imagine you are working for a children's charity. Design a poster to be displayed in public places such as bus stops and tube stations to highlight the plight of child marriage.

♦ In small groups design an app for a smartphone that highlights a children's rights issue. Your app should offer advice and help children who might be at risk. What will your app be called? Choose from one of the following topics:

- the right to privacy

- the right to education

- the right to clean air.

Oral

♦ As a class, discuss what rights you believe under 18s in the UK should have that they don't already.

♦ Divide the class into two and hold a debate about the legal age to vote in the UK. One half should make the case for it to be lowered to 16 and the other half should argue for it to remain at 18.

♦ 'Parents who share pictures of their children in social media are violating their child's privacy and putting their human rights at risk'. In small groups discuss this statement. Have your parents put images of you on the internet? How did this make you feel? What would you say to a parent who shares images of their child on social media?

Reading/writing

♦ Imagine you are the headmaster/headmistress of a secondary school in the UK. You are concerned about your students' online safety and decide to write a letter that will be sent home to parents. Create a draft letter, explaining the dangers of online grooming and warning signs they should look out for. You should also include advice on where parents can go to for help and support if they are worried about their child.

♦ Read the article *Girls Rights* (pages 13–14). Write a summary of the article, describing the 'double discrimination' girls face and in what ways girls are more discriminated against than boys.

♦ Write an article for your school/college newspaper explaining why it is important for children to be made aware of their rights. Include a list of organisations and websites children can visit for more information.

Acknowledgements

The publisher is grateful for permission to reproduce the material in this book. While every care has been taken to trace and acknowledge copyright, the publisher tenders its apology for any accidental infringement or where copyright has proved untraceable. The publisher would be pleased to come to a suitable arrangement in any such case with the rightful owner.

The material reproduced in **issues** books is provided as an educational resource only. The views, opinions and information contained within reprinted material in **issues** books do not necessarily represent those of Independence Educational Publishers and its employees.

Images

Cover image courtesy of iStock. All other images courtesy Freepik, Pixabay & Unsplash.

Additional acknowledgements

Page 8: From https://www.ohchr.org/en/stories/2021/07/childrens-right-privacy-digital-age-must-be-improved, accessed: 22 June 2022 © 2022 United Nations. Reprinted with the permission of the United Nations.

Page 39: From (https://news.un.org/en/story/2022/03/1114482, accessed 27 June 2022 © 2022 United Nations. Reprinted with the permission of the United Nations

With thanks to the Independence team: Shelley Baldry, Tracy Biram, Klaudia Sommer and Jackie Staines.

Danielle Lobban

Cambridge, September 2022